THE COMMON PEOPLE
OF COLONIAL AMERICA

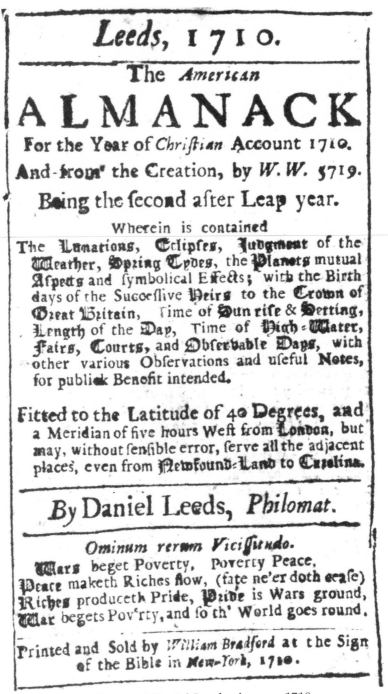

Leeds, 1710.

The *American*

ALMANACK

For the Year of *Christian* Account 1710.
And-from the Creation, by *W. W.* 5719.

Being the second after Leap year.

Wherein is contained

The Lunations, Eclipses, Judgment of the Weather, Spring Tydes, the Planets mutual Aspects and symbolical Effects; with the Birth days of the Successive Heirs to the Crown of Great Britain, Time of Sun rise & Setting, Length of the Day, Time of High-Water, Fairs, Courts, and Observable Days, with other various Observations and useful Notes, for publick Benefit intended.

Fitted to the Latitude of 40 Degrees, and a Meridian of five hours West from London, but may, without sensible error, serve all the adjacent places, even from Newfound-Land to Carolina.

By Daniel Leeds, *Philomat.*

Ominum rerum Vicissitudo.
Wars beget Poverty, Poverty Peace,
Peace maketh Riches flow, (fate ne'er doth cease)
Riches produceth Pride, Pride is Wars ground,
War begets Pov'rty, and so th' World goes round.

Printed and Sold by *William Bradford* at the Sign of the Bible in *New-York*, 1710.

Title page of Daniel Leeds *almanac, 1710.*

THE COMMON PEOPLE
OF COLONIAL AMERICA

*As glimpsed through the dusty Windows
of the old Almanacks, chiefly of New-York*

BY

LOUIS K. WECHSLER

5987

VANTAGE PRESS
New York   Washington   Atlanta   Hollywood

Published by Vantage Press, Inc.
516 West 34th Street, New York, New York 10001

Manufactured in the United States of America
Standard Book Number 533-03304-7

Library of Congress Catalog Card Number: 77-085411

For Toni

Contents

List of Illustrations

I'm come to tell many things good, and many things not so good; but the good and the bad in everything are all packed up together now-a-days. So here's my almanacks; they've cost no little labour, I'll assure ye. "Bless me," cried old Betty Winkle, "a man must have a monstrous long head, to make all these 'ere calculations!"—Ah, good woman, indeed he must. The head of an almanack-maker is nothing more nor less than a telescope, reaching from pole to pole, and of sufficient diameter to embrace the whole face of the heavens above, and the earth beneath! The firmament to him is a sort of checkerboard, and the earth a bowling-green! Come, who buys my wares? Here's the Sun, Moon and Stars all for sale!

("Tim Twilight," chapman, in *The Farmer's Almanac*, January, 1822.)

Introduction

The democratic spirit of the twentieth century has been reflected in the study of American literary history through a more respectful examination of what might be called subliterary sources. Early in the century Bliss Perry of Harvard recognized this tendency and stamped the seal of academic approval on it. "The historians of American literature," he wrote, "must ultimately reckon with all those sources of mental and emotional quickening which have yielded to our pioneer people a substitute for purely literary pleasures: . . . must picture the daily existence of our citizens from the beginning; their working ideas, their phrases and shibboleths and all their idols of the forum and the cave."

More than thirty years before Perry voiced this thought, Moses Coit Tyler, with characteristic acumen, had called the attention of his contemporaries to one of the most important of these subliterary sources, the Colonial almanacs, which in his day were overlooked by all but a few antiquarians as valuable material for students of American life and literature. One feels the enthusiasm and conviction of the pioneer in his memorable words:

> No one who would penetrate to the core of early American literature, and would read in it the secret history of the people in whose minds it took root and from whose minds it grew, may by any means turn away, in lofty literary scorn, from the almanac,—most despised, most prolific, most indispensable of books, which every man uses, and no man praises; the very quack, clown, packhorse, and Pariah of modern literature.

Once the trail had been opened by Tyler, others soon followed. In the last decade of the nineteenth century, the contents of the almanacs of Benjamin Franklin in Philadelphia and of Nathaniel Ames, father and son, in Boston were made available to the general public. In 1904, Kittredge published his delightful essays on the *Farmer's* almanacs of Robert B. Thomas begun in 1793. Clarence Brigham again called attention in 1925 to their value for historical study—a thesis confirmed ten years later by C. N. Greenough's article on New England almanacs in the decade before the American Revolution. Old almanacs were resurrected from cellars and attics, were sought by librarians in collections of uncatalogued bequests, and brought fancy prices at auctions—$50,000 over forty years ago for the rare first impression of the first *Poor Richard* (1733).

These early American almanacs have an added significance because the common people of that period, the farmers, artisans, and petty tradesmen, have left practically no written record of their thoughts. We can, therefore, find out what they were thinking about only indirectly, that is, through what they were reading. Fortunately, most of them could and did read.

Geographic and economic conditions limited their reading at that time mainly to the Bible and the almanac. Indeed, it is not far from the truth to state that the almanac was the secular Bible of the common people of Colonial America. Nathaniel Ames (1754) tells us that his almanac "enters the solitary dwellings of the poor and illiterate where the studied ingenuity of the learned writer never comes." Franklin, in his *Autobiography*, remarks that the almanac "was generally read, scarce any neighbourhood in the province being without it." Such circulation and publishing figures as we have bear witness to this fact. The *Ames* almanacs, the most popular of the eighteenth century, had an annual circulation of from 50,000 to 60,000 copies, to say nothing of the thousands of copies that were pirated. *Poor Richard* sold about 10,000 copies annually; and these were only two among many. Paul Leicester Ford observed that a "collection of the first issues of the early American presses established in the various towns, would, with hardly an exception, consist of these little waifs."

The conditions that gave the almanac this great predominance over all other secular books are a matter of common knowledge. Books were expensive, and, besides, as Ellery Channing wrote in describing the poor farmers of New England:

> Books to them
> Are the faint dreams of students, save that one—
> The battered Almanack—split to the core,
> Fly-blown and tattered, that above the fire
> Devoted smokes and furnishes the fates
> And perigees and apogees of moons.

Newspapers were not only expensive, but also difficult to distribute under Colonial conditions, and their circulation was, therefore, very limited. Poor or parsimonious farmers—and they constituted the great bulk of the people—could manage to get along without books and newspapers, but the almanac was indispensable in those days, when farms were widely scattered and isolated, and there were no calendars and very few clocks, and men believed strongly in the influence of the moon and stars on their daily lives. Perhaps the almanacs, inexpensive as they were, and great as the popular demand for secular reading was, might have been no more extensively sold than the cheap broadsides and chapbooks if they had not contained the "Man of Signs," the tables of zodiacal signs for each day of the month, and the weather predictions. We know that when John Holt, the revolutionary printer of New York, omitted the astrological and "meteorological" features in his *Freeman's New York Almanack* for 1767, the farmers refused to buy it, and he hastened to put them back, "although useless," in his next almanac. Consequently, there was sufficient demand for almanacs, as for cheap broadsides and chapbooks, to induce the itinerant peddlers of the time to carry them in stock together with the rest of their miscellaneous merchandise; and these peddlers, some time before New Year's Day, got them, somehow, to the settlers living in the most remote frontier districts.

Since calendars are all alike, enterprising printers and almanac-authors early sought to add special features in order to increase the sales of their own publications over those of their numerous competitors. In the sixteenth century the "prognostications" were included in the English almanacs. During the latter part of the seventeenth century the tempo of improvements was accelerated, and, by the middle of the eighteenth century, the Colonial almanac had become a miniature encyclopedia, a village library, a popular magazine and newspaper containing not only the regular elements of the almanac, but also editorials, poetry, essays, fables, anecdotes, excerpts from contemporary "best-sellers," the important news of the year, agricultural, medical, and culinary advice, scientific articles, and a miscellany of proverbs, jokes, riddles, paradoxes, questions and answers, beauty hints, statistics, and so forth. Some of the almanacs contained as many as 72 pages, so closely packed as to be equivalent to 100 normal book-pages; in a few cases, where the blank spaces were too narrow for horizontal lines, but sufficiently long, jokes and proverbs were filled in with lines arranged vertically. The varied contents of these almanacs provided a sort of practical and even liberal secular education for those who only other book was the Bible. In his preface to the almanac for 1765, Ames wrote:

> I have been very anxious to have . . . [this almanac] become as useful as possible to those whose Oracle is an Almanack, such as are destitute of any other Periodical Performance, as Magazines, or the like, or even News Papers.

And there were very many in this class, particularly in the frontier settlements, where the almanac was usually the only means of communication with the outside world. It is no wonder then that it was read again and again during the year and indelibly impressed on the minds and hearts of its readers. The study of these almanacs should, therefore, lead to a better understanding of the life and thought of the common people of those times.

The almanac-author was in the position of an editor. He printed either what he thought his readers would want to read or what he thought they ought to read. He was usually a man of the common people himself, or quite close to them, and understood their inclinations and aspirations. If he made a mistake in gauging his readers' tastes and needs, he soon heard from them, either by a letter of vigorous protest, or, what was worse, a disheartening silence. An example of the former type of response is the dispute between Roger Sherman, as almanac-author, and Henry De Foreest, his New York printer. It appears that De Foreest had inserted some Rabelaisian "observations" on the months and seasons in Sherman's almanac for 1750, without the author's permission, and these had offended many good Puritan customers and probably the author himself. Sherman thought the case important enough to write a letter to the *New York Gazette,* printed by De Foreest's rival, James Parker. In it he indignantly disclaimed authorship of the "prognostiferous" compositions. Peace was, apparently, patched up again between the two men, because *Sherman* almanacs were printed by De Foreest in New York for four years after the incident, but the De Foreest imprint did not appear on any almanacs after 1754. It is not improbable that the coarse language of those observations cost him a good many customers and had something to do with the cessation of his printing of almanacs. The mistake of John Holt in omitting the astrological and similar appendages of his almanac offers, on the other hand, an instance of the second type of control exercised by the common people over the almanacs. Although he intended to correct what he believed to be a ridiculous and harmful superstition, they were not yet ready to follow him, and by their tacit disapproval, expressed in the form of refusing to buy his almanacs, compelled him to yield to their wishes.

There is a special kind of reward in approaching the past through a contemporary record like the almanac. Some of the flavor of a bygone day can still be sampled, something of the comforting confusion and inconsistency which the historians, wise after the event, usually eliminate from their generalizations, a familiar glimpse of the past in its everyday aspect. Of this rare flavor the almanacs have more than their allotted share, partly because of the frequent use of their interleaved pages as diaries. The calendar pages, too, are frequently covered with notes of the weather for each day and interesting memoranda of important public events side by side with events in the lives of the owner and his family and friends. A *Roger More* almanac of New York for 1758, for example, records as of apparently equal importance the birth of a calf and the capture of Cape Breton by the English. Kept without an eye on posterity, these manuscript diaries are quite self-revealing, and freshen the dead past like a breeze that is let into a musty old attic through a long unopened window. Then again, there is the constant satisfaction of listening to the subtly different idiom of a vanished people, which revives the living temper of the age. These old almanacs often come close to the daily speech of the common man of their time, reflecting the popular idiom in a snatch of conversation, or the turn of a proverb, or a tart preface.

But much is lost by regarding the old almanac merely as a mirror of the activities and ideas of the common people. If we recall the revolution in thought which during the eighteenth century shifted the center of men's interests in this country from the religious to the secular aspects of life, and then consider that the almanac was the only important source of secular literature among the common people during that time, we discover a function of the almanac which has not been sufficiently stressed. The almanac contained not only information of immediate and practical value to its readers, but also much that served the purpose of opening their eyes to some of the momentous things that were going on in the world from which they were almost entirely shut off and about which they were as hungry for news as a traveller in a distant country longs for a letter from home. Unconsciously or deliberately, the almanac-author was satisfying a great need of the age and contributing a substantial share to the movement of secularization and democratization during this century.

We often come upon independence of thought and dignity among the rude people of the frontier, though it was difficult for them to communicate both with the world beyond the wilderness and with each other. Probably a part of the credit for this belongs to the circumstances under which they lived, but I believe part of it was also due to the influence of the almanac. It is not a mere accident that the library of Thousandacres, the heroic backwoodsman of Cooper's *Chainbearer*, consists of a *fragment* of a Bible, *Pilgrim's Progress*, and an almanac that was four years old. The men and women of the frontier, and those in the settlements, to a lesser extent, may have used the almanac by day for the practical tasks involved in making a homeland of a wilderness, but at night they found in it enough general information, refinement, beauty, and idealism to keep them from drifting away from civilization. The few pages of nonpractical poetry, history, geography, science, and philosophy which they received once a year counteracted to some extent the brutalizing and anarchic influences of Colonial life and partly took the place of school, newspaper, and neighbor as an educative and socializing force.

I am not sure that all the almanac-authors were conscious of this vital educative work that they were doing. Many of them undoubt-

edly were merely earning money by answering a certain popular demand, but the more intelligent of them realized this essential service
of the almanac and deliberately fostered it. Benjamin Franklin considered his *Poor Richard's Almanack* "a proper vehicle for conveying instruction among the common people, who bought scarce any other
books." The *Nathaniel Ames* and *Nathaniel Low* almanacs published in
Boston frequently reflected a didactic purpose. A New York almanac-
author, writing under the pseudonym of "Thomas More," revealed in
his almanac for 1746 that he had been ineffectually endeavoring for a
long time "to cure the Country-man of his rancid and inveterate disease of wrangling," which made lawyers rich at his expense.

This educational function of the almanac has been hardly more
than mentioned in passing. One phase of it, the part played by the
almanacs in cultivating revolutionary sentiment for independence
among the common people in the years before the war with England,
has received relatively more attention, but another phase has been
comparatively neglected, the fact that their minds had already been
fertilized before the seed of independence was planted. In this connection it is important to note that the censorship of almanacs in the
colonies was, fortunately, removed at about the beginning of the
eighteenth century, and that their logical development into organs of
popular education could go on unhampered by the authorities.

My examination of a representative selection of almanacs published in the other colonies indicates that the New York almanacs of
the period before the War for Independence (1694–1776) were fairly
typical. This is understandable since New York occupied culturally an
intermediate position between the cultures of New England and the
South and almanacs were widely sold to the north and south of the
province. The main difference that I have observed between the New
York and the New England almanacs is the greater coarseness of language and content in the former and the more serious tone of the latter. By comparison with the almanacs of the North, those of the
South generally contained less reading matter.

This book has been arranged in two parts. Part One, "Image of
the Common People," deals with the activities, attitudes, and opinions of the readers reflected in the almanacs. Part Two, "Education of
the Common People," focuses on the efforts of the almanac-authors
to advise their readers on personal and social problems and to extend
the boundaries of their interests and knowledge. I have used the term
almanac-author to signify the person or persons responsible for the
reading matter and policy of the almanac. His identity often cannot be
ascertained; he might be the compiler, or the printer, or both. Even
when his name is given, we cannot be sure that the printer is not hid-
ing behind it.

I have been liberal in quoting from the almanacs first because the
quality and flavor of their contents can be adequately conveyed in no

other way, and second because the old almanacs are not readily accessible to the general reader.

I must gratefully acknowledge the many courtesies extended to me by the New York Historical Society, the New York Public Library, the American Antiquarian Society, the American Philosophical Society, and the libraries of Columbia University, Harvard University, and Rutgers University. If I do not mention many others which were most helpful, it is not because they were less generous, but only because they happened to have less to offer.

I am deeply grateful to Professor Richard B. Morris of Columbia University for reading the manuscript and encouraging me to have this study published.

Part One

IMAGE OF THE COMMON PEOPLE

CHAPTER 1

The Colonial Almanacs of New York:
Their Authors and Printers

The title page of the *Daniel Leeds* almanac for 1694, the first almanac printed in New York, informed the reader that it was "chiefly accommodated to the Lat. of 40 degrees, but may without sensible error serve the Places adjacent, from Newfoundland to . . . Virginia." The latitude of forty degrees is a line passing a few miles north of Philadelphia, where the almanacs of Daniel Leeds had been published since 1687. The outlook of the author of the first New York almanac was not confined to this province, and the Colonial almanacs of New York generally expressed a broad, nonprovincial point of view. In fact, beginning with the issue of 1701, Daniel Leeds used the title, *The American Almanack*.

This is not surprising if we recall that the cosmopolitan seaport on Manhattan Island had a monopoly of printing in the colony until the Revolution. Nor was the city much less cosmopolitan in those days than now. The French Jesuit Jogues states that eighteen different languages were spoken in New Amsterdam as early as 1643;[1] a few years before the Revolution public worship in New York City was performed every Sunday in the English, Dutch, French, and German languages;[2] and Dutch almanacs were printed in New York for more than thirty years prior to the Revolution. It is also remarkable that of the eight most prominent printers of New York before the Revolution only one, Henry De Foreest, was born in New York,[3] and that four of them, Bradford, Parker, Holt, and Rivington were engaged in business in other colonies.

3

We have some ground for believing that the almanac-authors kept in mind the mixed character of their audience and sought as much as possible to arrive at a common denominator in their almanacs. I have already given examples in the cases of De Foreest and Holt of the effect of the failure to achieve this goal. There is also the instance of Daniel Leeds going so far in his Episcopalian zeal (after his conversion from the Quaker faith) as to refer to the Church of England as the "Christian Church." He immediately realized, however, that he was skating on thin ice, for he hastened to add that he did not mean that it was the only Christian church. He believed, indeed, that in their main tenets the Presbyterians, Independents, and "the better sort of Baptists" were Christians, but only the Episcopal bishops could claim "lawful Ordination by a regular Succession from Christ and his Apostles." Therefore, he concluded, he hoped that Christians would soon patch up their differences. The almanac-author had to step gingerly.

The Colonial almanacs printed in New York may be conveniently grouped into two periods, the Bradford Period, 1694–1744, and the Period of Expansion, 1745–1776. During the first period William Bradford was the only printer of New York almanacs. The twenty-four-page *Leeds* almanacs were the most popular and successful of this period. During the second period, no one printer succeeded in acquiring the control of the almanac output of the province that Bradford had possessed. There was much more competition, but, on the other hand, there was a much richer field in which to operate, for the colony was beginning to enjoy the fruits of more than a hundred years of battling with the wilderness. The most widely sold almanacs of this period were the *More* and *Hutchins* almanacs, the former identified with the name of the printer, James Parker, and the latter printed by Hugh Gaine. These two men were also the most successful printers of that period.

After 1776 New York City's monopoly of the printing of almanacs in this state ended, and, almanacs were printed in Fishkill, Albany, Hudson, Poughkeepsie, and Sag Harbor, Long Island.

The Bradford Period, 1694–1744

The establishment of the first printing press in New York by William Bradford is connected with the first notable skirmish over the freedom of the press in this country. Bradford, who had set up the first printing press in Pennsylvania near Philadelphia in 1685, was arrested in 1692 on a charge of anonymously printing a seditious pamphlet by George Keith, the celebrated Quaker apostle and apostate. He conducted his own defense so ably that the jury acquitted him and historians later conferred on him the honorable title of father of the freedom of the American press, but he was nevertheless very happy to accept the timely offer by Governor Fletcher of New York of the position of "Printer to King William and Queen Mary, at the City of New York," and began printing there in the spring of 1693. One of his first publications, naturally, was an almanac for the following year by Daniel Leeds, whose almanacs he had been printing annually in Philadelphia since the issue for 1687.[4]

Bradford, born in Leicestershire, England, May 30, 1663,[5] had been apprenticed to the Quaker printer, Andrew Sowles, in London, and at a very early age had espoused his master's daughter and faith. There is some confusion about the details of his migration to William Penn's new colony, but the most plausible explanation is that of John W. Wallace, who thought that he came over with Penn on the *Welcome* in 1682, made a survey of the country, returned to England, got married, and came back in 1685 with wife and press.[6] Before his trial in 1692, he had twice incurred the displeasure of the authorities, and, after the second affair, had been on the verge of returning to England. Only a change of front on their part induced him to stay.[7] He did not altogether sever his connection with the printing business in Philadelphia when he removed to New York, and is supposed to have had an interest in the press of Reinier Johnson from that time until his son, Andrew Bradford, took charge of it in 1712, and then in his son's business for many years thereafter. He followed George Keith into the Episcopalian fold, becoming a vestryman of Trinity Church in New York in 1703. On October 16, 1725 he commenced the publication of the *New York Gazette,* the first New York newspaper, which appeared under his management for about seventeen years. Another of his pioneer achievements was the founding of the first paper mill in America in 1690 at Roxboro, Pennsylvania. Besides Andrew, he had an older son, William, and a daughter, Facey. In his late sixties, soon after the death of his first wife, Elizabeth, he married a widow, Cornelia Smith, who had several children by her former husband. There is reason to believe that his second marriage was not altogether happy. He did not retire from business until he was close to eighty. He died just before his ninetieth birthday, on May 23, 1752. He seems to have been a man of strong mind and character, loyal in friendship, and not afraid of fighting against odds. Franklin describes him as "a crafty old sophister," but clearly reveals also that he went out of his way to be kind to the clever young exile from Puritan Boston.[8] His obituary in the *New York Gazette* is, therefore, probably true as well as appropriate when it says of him that he "was a man of great sobriety and industry; a real friend to the poor and needy, and kind and affable to all."[9]

The *Leeds* almanacs were the work of three members of that family, the father, Daniel, and two sons, Titan and Felix. Daniel Leeds prepared New York almanacs from 1694 to 1713. A copy of the almanac for 1706 in the John Carter Brown library differs from the only other known copy in that it contains a polemical essay of more than four thousand words on the Quaker religion. Titan Leeds continued the series from 1714 to 1744, interrupting it only in 1727. Felix Leeds's name appeared on almanacs for three years, 1727, 1728, and 1730.

The almanacs of Daniel Leeds are the most flavorsome of the three, reflecting a personality more vigorous than that of his sons. The influence of the Philadelphia origin of his almanacs continued to be felt in the New York editions. For example, the lists of roads in the almanac for 1695 use Philadelphia as the point of departure. In addition, Daniel Leeds seems to share the bitterness and animosity toward the Quaker authorities of Philadelphia which Bradford carried away with him to New York. These are revealed again and again in the pages of his almanacs until the hatchet was buried in the issue for 1711.

These early almanacs bear witness to the hard struggle of the early settlers. After all, the first of them bears a date only twelve years older than that of the founding of Philadelphia. The chronologies contain such reminders as: "141 Persons dyed in the County of Burlington," 1689; "Great flood at Delaware," 1691; "The Post Office erect. in America by Coll. Andrew Hamilton, from Boston to Virginia," 1694;[10] "Building of Trinity Church in New York," 1697 (the first); and "Last Hard Winter," 1698. The *Daniel Leeds* almanac for 1694 is, to my knowledge, the first American almanac that contains lists of the main highways from one center of population to another. That was only the fourth year after the opening of a colonial postal service. The *Ames* almanacs, which were started more than thirty years later and considered the best of their time, did not contain this feature for many years after the series began. We also catch a glimpse now and then of that amusing expression of nostalgia among immigrants which consists in disparaging familiar objects in the new country by comparison with similar ones in the "old country," as when a nameless versifier in the *Leeds* almanac for 1710 finds that the birds of this country, even the "Whip-poor-Will," do not equal the "British Birds" in their singing.

This pioneer world is reflected in the author of these almanacs. He tells us that he was born October 29, 1651,[11] the son of a poor mechanic who was unable to give him a good formal education.[12] His father, however, was descended from "a Gentlemen from Leeds in Kent," whose coat of arms "beareth Argent a Fess Guels [Gules] between Three Eagles Sable"[13] (i.e., white with red horizontal bar between three black eagles). This device was later displayed on the title page of his sons' almanacs.[14] He was living in 1705 in Egg Harbor, New Jersey.[15]

Common sense was his outstanding characteristic. While he was a Quaker for a time, he belonged to the militant faction who believed

Figure 1. Burgis View of New York from Long Island, 1717.

that it was their right and duty to use arms to defend themselves.[16] He also had a very sensible attitude toward his muse, whom he once addressed in the following spirit:

> Fly not too high my Genius, know thy Wings
> Weak-feather'd are, to soar to th'highest things;
> Undress'd and Unadorn'd is thy Quill;
> To please the Critick, deficient is thy skill.
> Let not thy fancy aim at things sublime,
> High flights do often times become a crime.[17]

In a fight he was a tough opponent, as an almanac-author of Philadelphia, Jacob Taylor, found out, whom he finally demolished by advising him not to crow "like a Cock on his own Dung-hill."[18] He was given to strong feelings and equally strong language, which, careless of the niceties of grammar and polite intercourse, has a fresh earthy quality. His proverbs, whatever the source, express his own taste. For instance, fanatical Christians were termed "Saints in the Church, but Goats in the Garden";[19] readers were reminded that "a close Mouth catches no flyes";[20] and bachelors were warned to "Chuse neither Women nor Linnin by candle light."[21] He retired from the labor of preparing almanacs after the issue for 1713, and died September 28, 1720, in his sixty-ninth year.[22]

It is interesting to compare the first New York almanac with the earliest extant almanac printed in the colonies, the *Danforth* almanac for 1646. The size and general appearance of the pages are not very different, but the contents are considerably enlarged in *Leeds*. His almanac consists of twelve leaves, that is, twenty-four pages. The year begins, as in *Danforth's*, with the month of March, although *Tulley's* almanac since the issue for 1687 had been marking January as the first month. Beside the English name of the month was the corresponding Hebrew name, a practice which was discontinued in the issue for 1704. It is impossible to tell whether the *Danforth* almanac had a preface by the author, like that of *Leeds*, since the first part of the unique copy is missing, but, for the rest, it lacks many other features of the *Leeds* almanacs: the verses at the top of the calendar pages; the weather predictions for each month; the advertisement of books; and the proverbs squeezed piecemeal into blank spaces on the calendar pages. Some of the features of the *Leeds* almanacs, as, for instance, the weather predictions, had appeared in preceding almanacs. Weather predictions were on the calendar pages of *Tulley's* almanac for 1687 and succeeding years. Others, like the verses and proverbs, were not universally adopted until much later. *John Jerman's* Philadelphia almanac for 1731, although one of its printers was the creator of *Poor Richard*, does not contain verses, and the *Ames* almanac for the same year has no proverbs. Indeed, Daniel Leeds seems to have been the first American almanac-author to use a combination of verses, weather predictions, proverbs, and lists of roads and highways— features which later in the eighteenth century were inseparable from Colonial almanacs.

Certain other features of his New York almanacs deserve mention. They gave the time and place of courts and fairs, predicted the eclipses of the year and their calculated effects, followed the old custom of placing cryptic phrases after certain days of the calendar to help their readers make decisions at critical moments, and offered the "Man of Signs" for the use of amateur astrologers, beginning in 1705—a monster that first raised its ugly head in *John Foster*'s almanac for 1678. Besides, much information was supplied that was designed to improve the bodies, minds, and souls of readers, such as information about the use of herbs, rules for good health, hints for farming, chronologies of important events, and religious instruction. In short, we find in the almanacs of *Daniel Leeds*, either full-grown or in embryonic form, the main elements of the eighteenth-century Colonial almanac. Furthermore, he laid down the lines along which the New York almanacs were to develop during that century. When his twenty-four-page almanac, under the pressure of popular demand, was supplanted in the second half of the century by a thirty-six-page almanac, no radical change occurred. There was merely an expansion of the main features of his almanacs.[23] The average price of the New York almanac during the century was sixpence, which, with allowance made for the difference in the value of money, probably represented a cost to the purchaser about the same as that of the *World Almanac* today. However, during the Revolution the price rose, *Bickerstaff*'s almanac for 1778, for instance, selling at a shilling.

Titan Leeds was said to have been sixteen years old when he took over the preparation of the *Leeds* almanacs.[24] He seems to have changed their spirit somewhat. More space was devoted to the fair sex, chiefly from the point of view of their dangerous seductiveness. In the spring the reader was told:

> . . . as you walk May flowers home to bring
> Learn to be Deaf when subtil Syrens sing.[25]

In summer, he was reminded that:

> The Weather's hot, days burning eye
> Doth make the earth in savour frye.
> Dick on the Hay doth tumble Nell,
> Whereby her belly comes to swell![26]

In place of his father's vigorous style and intensity of belief, one finds a mild aspect of conformity in politics and religion, a typical instance of which is the preface for 1722, in which Titan, referring to himself as "one of the Meanest" of the subjects of "his sacred Majesty," urges his readers not to cry over spilled milk nor to worry about the possibility of having no milk to spill, but to be wise and "submit to the Will and Pleasure of the Almighty" and to love and obey the king.

Titan Leeds did not publish an almanac in New York for 1727. The recriminations that followed are forerunners of the disputes and accusations that became frequent later in the century over the "pirating" of popular almanacs. According to William Bradford, Titan Leeds in 1725 had contracted, for a consideration duly paid, to prepare almanacs exclusively for him. In spite of this agreement, Titan Leeds had sold almanacs for 1727 and 1728 to Sam. Keimer, a Philadelphia rival. Thereupon, Bradford printed almanace for these years by Felix Leeds, Titan's brother. Keimer declared that they were spurious and printed an almanac for 1729 by Titan Leeds in Philadelphia. Bradford countered with *Titan's New Almanac* for 1729 in New York and challenged Keimer or anyone else to prove that it was not the genuine article. Bradford printed another *Felix Leeds* almanac, one for 1730; and then the fight was brought to a close by the departure of Keimer for Barbados. In 1731 Titan Leeds was back in the Bradford fold, where he remained until and beyond his death.

In 1733 he was in a different kind of trouble. In a Philadelphia almanac printed by B. Franklin, one Richard Saunders, humbly styling himself "Poor Richard," regretfully predicted the death of his dear friend Titan Leeds in that year. Leeds, apparently ignorant of the recent history of Swift's Bickerstaff and Partridge, fell into the trap, as the inventor of Poor Richard had hoped he would. When he joyfully announced in his almanac for 1734 that he was still alive and proceeded to pile coarse abuse on the head of Poor Richard for the lie, he learned that it was not as easy as he had thought to deny a printed announcement of one's death. Poor Richard simply replied that Titan Leeds must be dead, for his friend would never have used such rude language. Five years later Bradford gave the watchful Richard Saunders another opportunity. In the *Leeds* almanac for 1739, he informed the public of the death of Titan Leeds the year before, and added that, before dying, the author had prepared almanacs for the next seven years. Poor Richard slyly replied that the printer had finally been constrained to reveal the death of his friend, which had really taken place, as he had predicted, in 1733. Moreover, he even published a letter in which Titan's ghost indignantly denied that he had left behind almanacs for seven years. By this time, however, Bradford had learned his lesson, and, without deigning to reply to Poor Richard, printed the alleged almanacs for the seven promised years, ironically entitling the last one, *The Dead Man's Almanack, 1744.*

Besides printing the *Leeds* almanacs, Bradford printed almanacs by John Clapp (1697 and 1699); Daniel Travis (1709 and 1710);[27] "B. A.

Philo-Astro" (1723); John Hughes (1728); and William Birkett (1728–1743).

John Clapp was the first resident of New York to prepare an almanac printed in this city. He owned at that time an inn about two miles outside of town, but later moved to Rye in Westchester County. He was a person of some political influence, and, as a member of the Anti-Leislerian party, took an active part in the turbulent politics of the last decade of the century.[28] His almanacs were arranged somewhat differently from the *Leeds* almanacs, the calendar months being printed on alternate pages. Daniel Leeds arranged them on consecutive pages, except in 1704 and 1705, when the Clapp arrangement was followed. The calendar months were generally printed on alternate pages later in the century.

The *Travis* almanacs are quite inferior in appearance, size, and quality to the *Leeds* almanacs. They had only eight leaves, or sixteen pages, and contained very little supplementary reading matter such as verses, proverbs, and lists of roads.

The almanac of "B. A." for 1723 is notable for its interest in astronomy. The best feature of the issue was an essay of about twelve pages on the Copernican theory, which included the most recent measurements of astronomers.

No copy of the *Hughes* almanac has been found.

The almanacs of William Birkett represent the only other important series printed in New York during Bradford's period. Only two copies have been found, the almanacs for 1738 and 1743. The issue for 1738, the only one I have been able to examine, resembles the *Leeds* almanacs in appearance but contains more typographical errors. January was still noted as the eleventh month. Some space was devoted to "mathematical questions," a feature of that decade in the *Leeds* and *Poor Richard* almanacs.[29]

The Period of Expansion, 1745–1776

The importance of William Bradford in the history of New York printing during the eighteenth century may be summed up in the fact that after his retirement the printing business of the province, was, with one exception, nearly monopolized either by his apprentices or by their apprentices. John Peter Zenger, his only competitor before his retirement, had been his apprentice. Henry De Foreest had been an apprentice of either Bradford or Zenger. James Parker and William Weyman had worked in Bradford's shop, and Hugh Gaine and John Holt had learned the business from Parker. The only exception is James Rivington, who rose to prominence at the end of this period.

Competition was naturally keener and, in the absence of copyright laws, rather rough. The result was not lower prices, but

manacs (which I shall treat separately later) were issued bearing the name of *Poor Tom, Thomas Moore, Richard Moore, Roger More, R. More,* and *Poor Roger.* The printers of these almanacs were James Parker, William Weyman, and Hugh Gaine. According to Hutchins, the author of the *More* almanacs was Mr. Grew, who died about 1760.

The accusations and counter accusations among these three men over the allegedly unauthorized use of the *More* or *Moore* name are amusing after all these years, but they were a source of great bitterness at the time. Parker went so far, in attacking Weyman after their quarrel, as to declare pointedly: "What pity tis, that the old Proverb which says, 'Save a Thief from the Gallows, and he'll cut your Throat,' should be so often verified."[34] Gaine, after being accused of dishonesty by Weyman, reminded him of a different "old Proverb, viz. The bigest Whore, cries Whore first."[35]

James Parker was probably the most important New York printer of this period, owning presses in Woodbridge, New Jersey, where he had been born, in New Haven, Connecticut, and in New York City. He needed partners to help him run this extensive business, which included the publishing of the successful *New York Gazette,* started in January, 1742/1743. His relations with all of them terminated unsatisfactorily. I have already referred to his quarrel with Weyman in 1759. His nephew, Samuel Parker, stayed with him for only one year; and John Holt, after a disagreement, went into business for himself and commenced the publication of a rival newspaper, *The New York Journal,* in 1766. Parker has to his credit, however, the establishment of the first permanent printing office in New Jersey in 1751. He was twice involved in political trouble because of his liberalism, but he was no Zenger and in both cases saved his own neck by betraying the name of the author of the printed matter in dispute.

William Weyman, the son of an Episcopal clergyman, had been born in Philadelphia. After the severance of his partnership with Parker, he, too, began the publication of a rival newspaper, the *New York Gazette,* and engaged in the printing business, but his affairs did not prosper. He died in 1768.

John Holt was a Virginian. He had failed as a merchant in his native state and had migrated to New York to improve his fortunes. He printed the first Connecticut newspaper from 1755 to 1760. In the decade before the Revolution, he supported the young leaders of the American party. His newspaper, the *New York Journal,* was the platform from which they addressed their appeals to the Americans for patriotism and union. During the Revolution, he had to remove his press to Esopus (Kingston) and later to Poughkeepsie.

In 1767 appeared *Freeman's New York Almanack* "By the author of several pieces that have been publish'd under the name of *Freeman,*" and printed by Holt. The author was John Morin Scott, one of the leaders of the "Sons of Liberty," who had published several articles under that pseudonym in the *New York Gazette;* the *Freeman* almanac appeared annually for six years. The liberal spirit of the author and printer is reflected in it. A rational point of view is prevalent and to some extent transforms the traditional character of the almanac. In the first issue, a brave experiment was attempted, the exclusion of the astrological parts, but it was too radical and had to be given up. After the defeat, the almanac tried to please both the traditionalists and rationalists among its readers. The astrological signs and symbols and the rest of the venerable hocus-pocus were printed as in the other almanacs, but the next or the very same pages often contained ironic comments on their utter worthlessness and angry remarks about the stupid stubbornness of human nature. The compromise pleased neither the conservatives nor the liberals, and the almanac did not appear after 1772.

In addition to the abovementioned almanacs, there was a large number of almanacs which appeared only once or a few times. I list them in chronological order:

Almanac by George Christopher (1754–1755), printed by Hugh Gaine.

The American Ephemeris for 1757 by Jesse Parsons, printed by Parker and Weyman.

Almanac by W. Wing (1762–1764), printed by Samuel Brown. The issues for 1762 and 1764 are very interesting and are informed by a liberal spirit very similar to that of the later *Freeman* almanacs. Brown was the son-in-law of Henry De Foreest.

The New Jersey Almanack of "Copernicus Weather-Guesser" or William Ball (1768–1770), printed by James Parker.

The New York Almanack of "Mark Time" for 1774, printed by John Holt.

Merry Andrew's New Almanack (1774–1775), printed by John Anderson. Anderson was the partner of James Parker's son, Samuel F. Parker, in 1773.

Meanwell's Town and Country Almanack (1774–1775). The almanac for 1774 was printed by Robert Hodge and Fred. Shober. Hodge, a Scotchman by birth, and Shober, a German, had run a printing office together in Baltimore before they came to New York.

Rivington's New Almanack (1774–1775), printed by James Rivington.

The Family Almanac by "Copernicus" (1775–1776), printer unknown.

The New York and Country Almanack of "Dick Astronomer" for 1776, printed by Shober and Samuel Loudon. The latter, of Scotch birth, had previously been a ship chandler and bookseller in New York. He favored the American party and in 1776 began the publication of a Whig newspaper, *The New York Packet.*

Father Hutchins's almanac for 1776, printer not mentioned in imprint.

James Rivington is an interesting figure of the pre-Revolutionary period. After a career of dissipation and bankruptcy in London, he emigrated to this country in 1760. Within a few years of his arrival, he opened bookstores in New York, Philadelphia, and Boston, but went into bankruptcy again. In a few years we find him in the printing and newspaper business. His newspaper, ably conducted and taking at first a neutral position in the conflict between the colonies and England, prospered until the Revolution broke out. During the Revolution he was a rabid royalist. In 1800, before retiring, he went into bankruptcy for the third time. Isaiah Thomas presented a vivid sketch of him:

> He possessed good talents, polite manners, was well-informed. . . . He knew how to get money, and as well knew how to spend it; being facetious, companionable, and still fond of high living; but, like a man acquainted with the world, he distinguished the guests who were his best customers. . . . To the other qualities of a gentleman, he added benevolence, vivacity, and, with the exceptions already mentioned, punctuality in business.

Sheet Almanacs

I have referred in passing to special variations of the almanac which popular demand and keen competition produced during this period of expansion. The earliest of these was the "sheet almanac," a type familiar also in the seventeenth century. The first almanac of *Daniel Leeds*, printed in Philadelphia by William Bradford, was a sheet almanac. There is a record of only one New York sheet almanac in the Bradford period, one for 1736, which was printed by him. The next record mentions a sheet almanac for 1750, printed by James Parker. The sheet almanac, to judge by the specimens that have survived, was a broadside on which pages approximately the size of those of the average pocket almanac, i.e., two by four inches, were marked off. The sheets were pasted up on a convenient wall and torn off at the end of the year. It is this fact which accounts for their scarcity. Of those printed in New York before 1800, only three have been found, *Gaine's Universal Sheet Almanacks* for 1788, 1789, and 1790, all of them in the library of the New York Historical Society. One of the librarians there told me they had been found under one of the layers of wallpaper in the room of an old house. They are very much alike. The sheet for 1788, for instance, contains the twelve "calendar pages" and, in addition, eighteen "pages" of miscellaneous information such as the dates of court sessions, a general description of America, the officers of the government, and so forth. The only known printers of sheet almanacs in New York during this century were Bradford, Parker, Gaine, and Holt. After 1775, Gaine had a monopoly of their production.

Pocket Almanacs

The "pages" of the sheet almanac, cut and bound together, with several leaves interspersed for personal memoranda, constituted a "pocket almanac." The earliest record of a New York pocket almanac is of one printed by James Parker for 1748. The earliest that are extant are the pocket almanac of Jesse Parsons for 1755, which was printed by De Foreest, and Gaine's *New York Pocket Almanack* for the same year. The two most important series are those printed by Parker and his partners between 1748 and 1769, usually as the *Universal Pocket Almanack* by "Roger More," and those printed continuously by Hugh Gaine from 1755 to 1800, with the exception of the year 1756, as the *New York Pocket Almanack* by "Poor Tom," "Thomas Moore," or "Richard Moore." Of the two the Gaine series was much the better. Gaine's *New York Pocket Almanack* for 1757 contains valuable army lists, tables of population for North America and New York City, and lists of New York privateers in the war with France; the one for 1771 has a "Prospect of the City of New York" engraved on the page facing the title page; that for 1772 contains a daily MS record of the weather for the entire year. The copy of the *Universal Pocket Almanack* for 1758 in the Library of Congress includes MS notes by Richard Gibbons, who was a major in the 20th Regiment at the siege of "Louisbourg" in 1758 and later Chief Justice of Cape Breton.

Less well known pocket almanacs are:

American Pocket Almanack for 1764, probably printed by Samuel Brown in New York.

Rivington's pocket almanacs for 1774 and 1775, printed by James Rivington.

Merry Andrews pocket almanacs for 1775 and 1776, printed by John Anderson.

Almanac-Registers

From the simple lists and tables of the pocket almanac it was but a step to the elaborate statistical features of the almanac-register, which was the ancestor of the *World Almanac* type of the present. These registers first appeared on the eve of the Revolution. Gaine's *Universal Register* for 1775 declares that it was "the first of its kind that ever appear'd in this Province." The Gaine registers were published, with interruptions, until 1793. By comparison with either the ordinary almanac or the pocket almanac, they were very large, consisting of between 142 and 214 pages. Like the pocket almanacs, they were printed with blank interleaved pages for memoranda. The Library of Congress copy for 1775 contains interesting MS notes on its blank pages. The registers for 1775 and 1776 were evidently sympathetic to the American cause, but a change of attitude is evident in the issues between 1778 and 1782. There were no *Gaine* registers for some years after the end of the Revolution; when the issue for 1786 appeared, it contained a significant change in the subtitle from *American and British Kalendar* to *Columbian Kalendar*.

Dutch Almanacs

The cosmopolitan character of New York City is partly revealed in the printing of Dutch almanacs there from about 1738 to 1771. Capricious chance, however, has preserved a copy of *De Americaanse Almanacke* of "Thomas More" for 1754,[36] and an eight-page fragment of *De Americaanse Almanacke* of "Roger More" for 1761, and the fragment survived only because it was carelessly bound in a copy of *Roger More's* English almanac for that year in place of the corresponding English pages.[37]

In the two copies which have survived, the supplementary reading matter is not translated from the English almanacs for those years. The Dutch verses, proverbs, and other features are entirely different; the 1754 almanac, for instance, contains a summary in Dutch of the "Constitution of the Seven United Provinces" not printed in the English edition. The general tone of these Dutch almanacs is more pious than that of their English cousins, particularly in the case of the proverbs, which are mostly devout exhortations on virtue rather than gems of worldly wisdom, as in the English. The plan and the arrangement are, however, identical.

The Revolution at first tended to curtail the output of almanacs in New York. The records mention eight different almanacs printed in the year before the outbreak of hostilities, and only two in the first year of the war. Furthermore, owing to the British occupation of the city, the rebel printers, like John Holt and Samuel Loudon, had to remove their presses to outlying districts and restrict their production to the most essential printing needs of the American party; the almanacs had to wait for a while. John Holt removed his press in 1776 to Esopus (Kingston), and the next year to Poughkeepsie. Samuel Loudon took his press to Fishkill. They, and others like them, thus encouraged the diffusion of the knowledge of the art of printing and broke up the monopoly of the business which New York City had retained until then.

Illustrations

Illustrations in almanacs, as in other periodicals, were very rare during the eighteenth century; and only one New York almanac can honestly be termed an "illustrated almanac," *Father Abraham's Almanack* for 1759, printed by Hugh Gaine. The idea did not "take," probably because the illustrations involved too great an expense for a publication that sold for sixpence. That the same reason operated in the higher-priced magazine field is instanced by the failure of Isaiah Thomas's attempt to found an illustrated magazine, the *Royal American*, in 1774. The first permanent New York illustrated periodical was the *New York Magazine* (1790–1797); illustrated almanacs, however, did not become general until the nineteenth century.

Before 1759 there was little in the way of embellishment in the almanacs aside from the crude figure of the Man of Signs, and an occasional cut on the title page. The engraving of the Man of Signs improved very slowly in quality; during the second half of the century, he sometimes appeared surrounded by the pictorial symbols of the twelve signs, for example, a bull for Taurus, a pair of scales for Libra, and so forth.

Father Abraham's Almanack for 1759 contains a plan of the harbor of "Louisburg"; a folding plate of Frederick the Great; an engraving, *The Astronomer*; illustrations for an account of the author's travels; and representations of the months. The plate of Frederick bears the inscription, "J. M. Ae. 14," and may have been the work of one of the apprentices of the Philadelphia engraver James Turner.[38] The engraving of the astronomer, signed "H. D.," is perhaps the work of the notorious Henry Dawkins, the wood engraver of Philadelphia and New York, who was arrested during the Revolution on a charge of printing counterfeit money in collaboration with the Tory printer James Rivington.[39] Dawkins's engraving *Urania* resembles *The Astronomer* in theme and treatment.[40] The representations for the months are similar to those which, since early times, and particularly during the Middle Ages, were used to adorn not only almanacs, but also manuscripts, books, and churches.[41] The plan of "Louisbourg" was included in *Poor Tom's* pocket almanac for 1759; and the plate of Frederick the Great and the plan appeared in the *Hutchins* almanac for the same year. A plan of Quebec was bound with the *Roger More* and *Thomas More* almanacs for 1760. The *Hutchins* almanacs for 1760 and 1761 contain woodcuts representing each month. Popular interest in the war with France was one of the inducements that persuaded the printer to add this expensive feature to the almanac.

Advertisements

In spite of their extensive circulation, the almanacs contained very few advertisements. Most of these were inserted by the printer himself, advertising books and stationery supplies, or offering cash for linen rags, and would be of interest mainly to those readers living near the printing office. I noted only five advertisements of other businessmen, two of which are by the same man, and three by businesses outside of New York.[42]

The association of patent medicine with the almanacs is a very old one. In fact, many of the early almanac-authors were quack doctors who used the almanacs to sell their fake medicines. Francis Moore, the founder of a long line of popular almanacs under that name, described himself as a "licens'd physician and student in astrology."[43] In New York the printers themselves were the distributors of patent medicines and advertised them and their curative properties rather often. Bradford sold "Lockyer's Universal Pill," which was very popular in England and this country in the latter part of the seventeenth century, and claimed to cure no less than "Agues, Feavers, Scurvey, Gout, Dropsie, Jaundice, Bloody Flux, Griping in the Guts, Worms of all sorts, the Gravel, Stone, Collick, and *many other Diseases*" (italics my own).[44] Other popular medicines of the time sold by New York printers were "Turlington's Balsam of Life";[45] "Dr. Radcliff's only true specific Tincture for the Tooth Ach";[46] "Stoughton's Bitters";[47] "Essence of the Balm of Gilead, or Nature's grand Restorative";[48] and "Dr. Ward's Essence for the Headach."[49] Dr. Radcliff's preparation, it was claimed, "gives immediate Ease in the most violent and tormenting Pain . . . and by constant using, never fails to prevent its Return! At once or twice using, it makes the foulest Teeth most beautifully White, assuredly fastens those that are loose, and infallibly preserves the Teeth from growing Rotten, and those a little decayed, from growing worse." Of the same truthful character are the advertisements of various beautifying preparations. A typical one sold by Hugh Gaine was "The Princely beautifying Lotion," which was guaranteed "infallibly" to take away wrinkles and smallpox pits and to make "those Persons, who before looked hagged and old, to look young, beautiful and fair."[50]

Correspondents

The relationship existing between almanac-author and reader during those years is clarified by considering the correspondence printed in the almanacs. Most of the letters are of an informational type intended for the use of the readers. They usually contained home recipes on culinary, cosmetic, agricultural, and medical matters. In the years before the Revolution, recipes for making native substitutes for imported beers and wines were eagerly sought and frequently submitted. Now and then, letters of approbation or protest were received, such as those Daniel Leeds received because of his caustic comments on the Quakers.[51] When the "mathematical questions" were a popular feature of the almanacs in the 1730s, answers were received from many readers. Men of the caliber of Thomas Godfrey of Philadelphia, inventor of the mariner's quadrant, and the missionary Reverend James Wetmore of Trinity Church in New York interested themselves in trying to solve the problems, and there was rivalry between almanacs in finding the most difficult problems.[52] Finally, there were sometimes letters telling about interesting experiences, such as the one in *Greenleaf's* almanac for 1792 describing the ceremony of crossing the tropic. On the other side, the almanac-author might ask his readers for their opinion in a matter of policy on which they seemed divided, as when Titan Leeds asked them whether he should continue to print verses at the top of each calendar page, after receiving letters from a few of his extremely pedestrian readers objecting to the waste of such valuable space.[53] In general, communication between reader and almanac-author was on a practical basis, the author acting as a kind of clearinghouse for the benefit of the readers.

MS Notes

The MS notes found in many of the almanacs are not an integral part of the almanac and yet add a special value and flavor to particular copies. They consist mainly of exercises in penmanship, notations of the weather, records of business transactions, and diaries. The *New York Pocket Almanack* for 1772 (New York Historical Society) contains a day-by-day record of the weather for the entire year. The diaries vary according to the character and ability of the diarists. Some, like the one in the *Roger More* almanac for 1758 (New York Historical Society), are of a simple objective kind, being confined to brief memoranda on the calendar pages, such as "Sick," "Calf," "fight," "Barn raise," "C Breton taken," "snow," "Church," and "Mr. Hooker married." Others go into somewhat more detail: "commenced board at Wattes," and "Diana began to wash for me."[54] One contemporary point of view is revealed in: ". . . [bet] a hat with T W M that the congress do not declare for Indepency in 4 Mo if they do not, I win—"[55] Entries of a more intimate nature are illustrated by this romantic confession: "30th July wrot to Phe[be] by Capt. Webly, the 5th letter to D[ate]: August 6th wrote her to write . . . if she has any affection for me if silent I consider it wanting . . . Nov—1th wrote 6th letter . . . direct to Pheebe—,"[56] and by this poignant record: "My dear Fanny departed this life on Wednesday 13 Sept. ½ hour after 3 in the morning. Aged 7 years 6 month 3 days."[57] An interesting diary entry is to be found in the Library of Congress copy of Gaine's *Universal Register* for 1775:

> By order of Congress an attempt was made to remove the Cannon from the Battery wch was watched by the Asia's Barge: The Barge fired on our People who returned the Fire & killed one Man in the Barge, then the Man of War fired, 24 Pounder 18 Pounder 9 Pounder & Grape & Swivel Shot. Three of our Men were wounded slightly, & a Number of Houses near the Battery were damaged. This Fracas began about ½ past 12 at night of the 23d & continued (with Intermissions) till 2 oclock in the morning of the 24th. The citizens removed 21 eighteen Pounders on Carriages, & all the Apparatus belonging to them. [August 24, 1775].

As we look back over the printing of almanacs in New York before the Revolution, we are struck by the fact that their history parallels the development of the province and the other colonies during those years. In the first period, the pioneer and the wilderness were still prominent factors in the life of the people. The pioneer printer, William Bradford, and the pioneer almanac-author, Daniel Leeds, dominated the almanac field, and the *Daniel Leeds* almanacs laid down the trail which the succeeding almanacs of the century were to follow.

The second period, approximately marking the midcentury, was one of swift expansion and intensified competition both in the province and in the almanac field. However, the link with the preceding pioneer period is very close, as we saw, for the leading printer of the period, James Parker, was a former apprentice of Bradford, and his chief competitor, Hugh Gaine, was his own former apprentice. Parker and Gaine printed the most successful almanacs of the time, the former printing the *More* almanacs and Gaine the *Hutchins* almanacs, which were the more popular of the two and continued to appear under Hutchins's name for more than seventy-five years after his death. The spirit of growth and rivalry was further manifested in the development of useful variations of the ordinary almanac: sheet almanacs; pocket almanacs, of which Gaine's *New York Pocket Almanack* was the best; almanac-registers, which Gaine was the first to print in New York and which are the progenitors of the modern *World Almanac* type; and Dutch almanacs, appearing until just before the Revolution, when the profitable demand for them ceased.

If we look ahead briefly to the period starting with the war for independence and ending with the first administration of George Washington we find that the monopoly of the printing of almanacs, which New York City had held from the beginning until the Revolution, was broken with the printing of almanacs in Fishkill, Albany, Hudson, Poughkeepsie, and Sag Harbor; and in 1785 an Albany almanac, the *Webster's Calendar,* began its long career of more than a century. As one would expect, the old landmarks, excepting the very adaptable Hugh Gaine, were swept away, and new printers and authors entered the field, patriotically begetting "Continental," "Columbian," and "United States" almanacs, and breathing the pride of country and the unbounded faith and hope in the new nation that were to subdue a continent in the next century.

CHAPTER 2

The New World

The Red Man

One factor which the settlers of the wilderness could not disregard was the American Indian. It is idle to speculate on what might have been the history of the relations between the aborigines and the colonists if the first comers had been as decent and intelligent as William Penn. They were not; and they, and all those who came after them, reaped a harvest of hatred and violence. To the Indian, the white man became an avaricious cheat who had come to steal his inheritance; to the white man the Indian was a vindictive heathen always looking for a chance to murder him and his family and standing in the way of progress. Innocent people on both sides suffered because of the bitter conflict between the two races and added the frenzy of unmerited injury to the deep-seated enmity inherited from the past.

It is, therefore, worth noting that New York almanacs contain only two references to the Indians before the period of the war with France. There is a brief allusion in the *Daniel Leeds* almanac for 1700 to the good fortune of the inhabitants of the Delaware River country in being free from the danger of Indian attacks, and another in the almanac for 1706 attempting to discredit the Indian policy of the Quakers. The 1700 almanac, which thanks "a special Providence" for placing them near the Delaware Indians, who were a "mixt decaying and beggarly People and so not capable of uniting in a Body to do us mischief," gives us the clue, I believe, to the long silence of the almanacs respecting the Indians. Chance, the kindness and fairness of Penn, the sensible Indian policy of the Dutch, and the feud between the Iroquois and the French—these had combined to reduce the danger of Indian hostility in the middle colonies during the first half of the eighteenth century, a state of affairs reflected in the New York almanacs by the striking paucity of material on the Indians until after the war with France.

24

The war with France ushered in a new era. The sons and successors of William Penn had alienated the Indians by disregarding the example of the founder of the colony, and their resentment quickly yielded to French encouragement. The almanacs soon reflected the changed state of affairs. The first story of Indian atrocity appearing in a New York almanac is a "true Relation of the unheard of Suffering of David Menzies, Surgeon, among the Cherokees," which was printed in *Roger More*, 1765. Dr. Menzies had been captured while attending some sick Negroes in a settlement on a branch of the Savannah River. He found that he was fated to expiate the murder of one of the Cherokee chiefs by white men.

> These Indians in one of their late incursions into South Carolina had met, it seems, with some larded venison, which hit their taste; in consequence whereof they had carried off some larding-pins as well as a quantity of bacon, and my cannibal mistress determined, by my means, an application of this discovery to human flesh. It was evening, and these barbarians brought me stark-naked before a large fire . . . and two young torturers, having fast-bound me to a stake, began to experiment on me the culinary operation of larding. After those Cooks of Hell had larded all my left side they turned it close to the fire, and proceeded on the other, . . . in reality a very painful process to a live creature, the pin not merely going through the insensible epidermis, or scarf-skin, but lacerating also the pyramidal papillae of the true skin, which anatomists agree to be the seat of feeling. [Luckily most of the savages by this time were either drunk or asleep.] I did not let this providential opportunity slip, you'll believe, but instantly disengaged my right arm (at the expence of the greater part of the belly of the palmaris brevis muscle, and with the dislocation of the eighth bone of the carpus) and fell to untying myself with expedition.

Before escaping, however, he placed firebrands among the tents of the Indians and soon had the satisfaction of seeing them in flames. He supported life in the wilderness with some bacon, which he had had the good sense to take with him before his escape, and which was "saturated with the juices" of his own body.

> And I am satisfied that I should have looked on an attempt to have deprived me of my Indian larding so much in the light of a robbery, as to have punished even with unlicensed death, any invader of my dearly acquired property.

He finally reached Augusta, where he remained with Justice Ray until his recovery from the experience. Physician to the end, he concluded with the admission that, since his being "larded," he had not suffered from a paralytic complaint in the roasted left side. It's an ill wind.

The atrocity story which was included in the *Hutchins* almanac for 1769 under the title, "A most remarkable Piece of inhuman Barbarity committed by some French and Indians, on one of the Dionandadies, for making Peace with the Five Nations about the Year 1695," is a gruesome masterpiece of its kind and in my opinion belongs with the famous passage in James Adair's *History of the American Indians,*[1] which many historians have conceded to be "the best description extant of torture at the stake":[2]

> The Prisoner being first made fast to a stake, so as to have room to move round it; a Frenchman began the horrid Tragedy, by broiling the Flesh of the Prisoner's Legs, from his Toes to his knees, with the red-hot Barrel of a Gun. His example was followed by an Utawawa, who being desirous to outdo the French in their refined Cruelty split a Furrow from the Prisoner's Shoulder to his Garter, and filling it with Gun Powder, set fire to it. This gave him exquisite Pain, and raised excessive Laughter in his Tormentors. When they found his Throat so much parched that he was no longer able to gratify their Ears with his Howling, they gave him water, to enable him to continue their Pleasure longer. But at last his Strength failing, an Utawawa slead of his Scalp, and threw burning hot Coals on his Scull. Then they untied him, and bid him run away for his Life. He began to run, tumbling like a drunken man. They shut up the Way to the East and made him run Westward, the Country, as they think, of departed miserable Souls. He had still Force left to throw Stones, till they put an End to his Misery by knocking him on the Head. After this, every one cut a Slice from his Body to conclude the Tragedy with a Feast.

In view of the state of mind which such stories cultivated, we can understand why the colonists of Pennsylvania and New Jersey who were not of the Quaker faith felt that the Quaker principles regarding the use of force were a menace to those colonies. The danger was not altogether of Indian origin. The abovementioned passage in the *Daniel Leeds* almanac for 1706 repeats the charge that the "Sweeds" or Dutch told the Indians, when the Quakers first settled in Burlington, that the settlers would not fight on principle, and that therefore they were free to kill them and take away their property, but the Indians apparently were not civilized enough to make an unprovoked attack.

It is wrong, however, to assume that there was no recognition at all among the colonists of the many injustices that had been committed against the Indians. There is some evidence in the almanacs of an attitude of sympathy and fairness, particularly among honest men who had been brought by circumstance into direct contact with the Indians and had been permitted to live among them. The men, for example, who negotitated a treaty of peace with the Indians near Lake Erie and the Ohio River tried to be fair according to their lights. One of the provisions of the treaty stated that an Indian who had killed an Englishman was to be tried by English laws, but the jury must be half Indian.[3] One of the almanacs contained an interesting discussion of the Indian problem from the colonists' point of view.[4] The writer pointed out a fundamental dilemma which faced the white settlers. If they were to live in peace and security, they must conquer the Indians. On the other hand, complete conquest would deprive the conquerors of the existing advantages of trading with them. He, therefore, offered this solution of the difficulty. Following the conclusion of a just, but firm peace with them, the colonists would offer a reward for every Indian child or young woman brought alive to them. The children would be placed in a "publick Seminary," where they "should be carefully brought up, instructed in the pure Doctrines of Christianity, the Practice of social Virtues, and at a proper Age taught useful Trades." The young women were to be confined only to the extent of preventing their returning home. They should be treated kindly and usefully employed. If they behaved properly and became civilized, "it should not be dishonourable for white Men to marry them." In fact, they would receive a small portion from the government on their marriage. What portionless white maidens would have to say about such unfair competition is not mentioned, but the suggestion is interesting as an early instance of the absence of prejudice against intermarriage with the Indians.

The *Roger More* almanac for 1767 quoted from the chapter on the Indians in the recently published *Concise Account of North America* by Major Robert Rogers, the famous American frontier fighter who had acquired an intimate knowledge of their manners, customs, and language in his early years, when he lived near them in a frontier settlement. The communal life of some of the tribes is described and then contrasted with that of the Christianized Indians. Rogers wrote:

> It is observable that in proportion as they lay by their savage customs, and conform to our methods of living, they dwindle away, either because these Methods are disagreeable and noxious to their constitutions, or else (which I am inclin'd to believe is the case) when settled among the English, they have greater opportunities of

procuring spirituous liquors, of which they are generally, male and female, inordinately fond; and very little care has ever been taken to prevent those, who are inclined to take advantage of them in Trade, from debauching them.

Major Rogers also explained why the use of Indians as slaves never was profitable:

The great and fundamental principles of their policy are that every man is naturally free and independent; that no one . . . on earth has any right to deprive him of his freedom and independency, and that nothing can be a compensation for the loss of it.[5]

A large part of the summary is taken up with the story of "Ponteack," the king of a great number of tribes around Lake Huron and Lake Michigan, and the most powerful Indian chief on the continent at that time. Rogers had first met him in 1760 while leading a party into his country. Had not Pontiac protected him and his party at that time, they would all have been killed by hostile Indians. Rogers had several conferences with him and came away from them with a profound admiration for his character and abilities. Observing Pontiac's great power, he tried to persuade the British government that it was in their interest to humor him and form an alliance with him, but they did not follow his advice. The consequence was the great Pontiac conspiracy of 1763, which almost succeeded in driving the English out of the Northwest territory.

So deep was the impression made by the Indian leader on Rogers that he published a play in blank verse about him, *Ponteack; or the Savages of America. A Tragedy* (1766), which has the honor of being our first play about the Indian. The plot, based on the conspiracy of Pontiac, illustrated two themes, the cheating of the Indian by Indian traders and his passionate devotion to the principle of revenge. The play was obviously not intended for the stage; the characters are cardboard figures who speak solemnly. Over all broods the calm and noble spirit of Pontiac. That there was a real basis for Rogers's view of his greatness of character is illustrated by this story, which the author can best tell in his own words:

In the year 1763, when I went to throw provisions into the garrison at Detroit, I sent this Indian [Pontiac] a bottle of brandy by a Frenchman: His counsellors advised him not to taste it, insinuating that it was poisoned, and sent with a design to kill him; but Ponteack, with a nobleness of mind, laughed at their suspicions, saying, it was not in my power to kill him, who had so lately saved my life.

Along with the atrocity stories, I found sentimental tales which represented the Indian as a "noble savage."[6] Examples of the sentimental type are the "Adventure of a young English officer among the Abenakee Savages,"[7] and the story of the Chactaw father.[8] The father offered himself in place of his son, who was about to be executed for the murder of a fellow tribesman, and was beheaded in his stead. The English officer was saved from death at the hands of the Indians by an old Indian whom he reminded of his own slain son and who took him back to the Indian village where he remained under his protection for several months. In the spring, before an Indian attack on the camp of the officer's former comrades, the old father asked him whether he could lift up the hatchet against the Indians with whom he had been living, to which the officer replied that, while he would never fight against the English, he would always look upon the Abenakees as his brothers. The old man, then, for the first time spoke to him of his dead son.

> His eyes looked wild, but no tears came from them. . . . He grew calm, and turning towards the East, he pointed to the rising Sun, and said to the young Englishman, "Seest Thou yon beauteous luminary, the sun, in all its splendor? Does the sight of it afford thee any pleasure?—Undoubtedly—And yet to me it no longer gives any! See, young man, does not that gay appearance of flower give thee a sort of joy to look at it?—It does indeed.—And yet it delights not me," adding with some degree of impetuosity, "Depart, haste, fly to yon camp of thy friends. Get home, that thy father may still see with pleasure the rising of the sun, and the flowers of the spring."

The Indian, as we find him in the New York almanacs, is a very serious person, whether as foe or injured neighbor. The lighter and less formal side of him, which we know existed when he was at play or in private conversation or elated by alcohol, is generally ignored, and I have come across only one instance of it, in an almanac near the end of the century, in which I read that an Indian chief compared a cask of Madeira to a juice extracted from women's tongues and lions' hearts. When he was asked to make himself clear, he added that the wine could make him talk forever and fight the devil himself.[9]

Indian Trails

It is well known that the main routes of travel used by the colonists were old Indian trails; and when Daniel Leeds published his first list of roads in the almanac for 1695, a "road" still represented often little more than a trail marked by blazed trees. The coaches which are popularly associated with colonial travel did not become a common sight on the roads until about the middle of the next century. Indeed, a hackney coach was seen in New York City for the first time a year after Daniel Leeds's list was made public;[10] and wheeled vehicles of any kind were extremely scarce throughout the colonies. The good people of Boston still entertained a strong prejudice against the recently introduced horse-coaches and considered them as "contrivances fit for this world only," which the righteous quite properly scorned.[11]

The time at which a traveller set out was determined by his own convenience, and the time of his arrival by chance, and, to some extent, by his own desire. Periodicity and regularity of transportation were as yet unknown. A postal service had been in operation between Massachusetts and Pennsylvania since 1691, and we can get a notion of the quality of the service at this stage if we recall that in 1753, when Franklin and Hunter assumed control of it, the time for sending a letter from Boston to Philadelphia was six weeks, and during the winter the mail started out only twice a month. Moreover, the Southern colonies did not enter the postal system until 1732.

Boston then was much farther away in time from New York than London is today, the trip taking at least seven days;[12] and travel south of Philadelphia during the first half of the eighteenth century was even more uncomfortable and slower than in the North. The *Thomas More* almanac for 1748 cautioned its readers about travelling in the South. They were by all means to avoid the eastern or shorter route southward through Chesapeake Bay because of the "Difficulty, Danger, and Dearness" in crossing the bay, and the "poor Accomodations both for Man and Horse." In general, the reader was advised that "thro' all Virginia and Maryland you generally met with but extraordinary ordinary Entertainment, and that at an excessive dear Rate." Besides this, the roads were very dry in the dry season and very muddy in the rainy season. This, however, was only half the picture, for the Southerner, of whatever degree, knowing that taverns were scarce and generally bad, hospitably received the wayfarer at any time of night or day and shared his best with him. Some planters even kept slaves along the highway whose duty it was to invite the passing traveller to be their master's guest for the night.[13] So we read in the *Virginia Almanack* for 1753 on the December calendar page:

Now let the weary Traveller be received with double

Welcome, and your best Liquors and Christmas Pies be
set for his Repast.

A very rapid general improvement of means of communication
and transportation began at about the time of the war with France.
Benjamin Franklin and the war probably had a good deal to do with
it. Soon after he was appointed postmaster general, the time for sending a letter from Philadelphia to Boston was cut from six to three
weeks, and weekly posts were established. In 1757 a semiweekly service was instituted between New York and Philadelphia. Nine years
later, mail left for Philadelphia three times weekly, for Boston twice
weekly, and for Albany and Quebec once weekly.[14] The effect of
these improvements was to increase the use of the mails and encourage the growth of good inns. The war, at the same time, tended to
improve the road system. Consequently, the time of the trip from
New York to Philadelphia, which was five days in 1750, was reduced
in 1756 to three days, and in 1771 to less than two days.[15] An advertisement in the *Thomas More* almanac for 1760 reveals a busy traffic
between New York and Philadelphia. The Burlington and Bordentown
boats left Whitehall Mondays and Tuesdays and arrived in Philadelphia, "Wind and Weather permitting," on the third day; the fare for
the through-trip was 6s1d. The Blazing-Star boats, leaving Whitehall
on Sundays and Wednesdays and making about the same time, were
more expensive, the fare being 9s. The former company carried the
passenger from Amboy to Bordentown or Burlington "in a waggon."
The fastest "de luxe" coachline to Philadelphia before the Revolution
was advertised in the *New York Pocket Almanack* for 1773 as follows:

> The Flying Machine, kept by John Mercereau, at the
> New-Blazing-Star-Ferry, near New York, sets off from
> Powles Hook every Monday, Wednesday and Friday
> Mornings for Philadelphia, and performs the Journey in
> two days (till the 1st of November). . . . The Waggons in
> Philadelphia set out from the House of Mr. Joseph Van-
> degrist, the same Morning. As the Stages set off early in
> the Morning, Passengers would do well to cross the
> Ferry the Evening before. The Price for each passenger is
> 20s.

In this period, too, almanacs began to include the secondary
roads in their lists,[16] and even the French routes from the mouth of
the St. Lawrence to the Mississippi[17] and from Montreal to Quebec.[18]
The lists of roads frequently included postal information. It is interesting to note that the Montreal-Quebec route was printed in French,
and also contained the "noms des Maitres des Postes, Noms des
Postes, Distance de Poste en Poste en Lieues, droit de voiture en Ar-

gent Halifax, En Argent courant, En Livres." It is the only French to be found in the New York almanacs before the "Calendrier pour l'an-nee sextile, la troisieme de la Republique Francaise" of 1794–5. In *Webster's Calendar* for 1793 I came across the first "Roads into Western Country."

The road lists in some of the almanacs are especially valuable because they add the post-stages and the names of their proprietors. *Freeman's* almanac for 1768 has a list of them on the Boston Post Road from New York to Hartford:

Post-stages, New York to Hartford, 1768:

Kingsbridge	Dyckman
East Chester	Butler
New Rochelle	Badow
Rye	Wright
Horseneck	Knap
Stamford	Quintard
Norwalk	Quintard
Fairfield	Burr's
Stratford	Benjamin's
Milford	Bryan's
New Haven	Beers
Wallingford	Johnson's
Durham	Not known
Middletown	Shaylor
Weathersfield	Kilbourn
Hartford	Bullor and Butler

Hutchins almanac for 1772 contains post-stages to Albany on the west side of "Hudson's River." West post-stages, New York to Albany, 1772:

Dunmere's	16mi. (Hackensack)
Hopper's	10mi.
Slut's	14mi.
Yeoman's	15mi.
Mandevel's	10mi.
Merrit's	10mi.
Devoe's	14mi.
Bogardus's	12mi.
Snyder's	12mi.
Brando's	8mi.
Hornbeck's	14mi.
Widow Vernon's	24mi. (Albany)

Incidentally, this list illustrates the practice of calculating distances in Colonial times between taverns rather than between towns. *Rivington's* pocket almanac for 1774 gives the stages on the east side of the river. East post-stages, New York to Albany, 1774:

Busson's	15mi.
Owdel's	12mi.
Capt. Purdy's	12mi.
Peck's Kill	10mi.
Warner's	6mi.
Haight's	12mi.
Fish-Hills	3mi.
Brewer's Mills	6mi.
Poughkeepsie	8mi.
Barracks	12mi.
Capt. Taller's	10mi.
Livingston's Manor	10mi.
Capt. Conyn's	10mi.
Widow Van Allen's	9 mi.
Kinderhook	6 mi.
Fitch's	12mi.
Albany	9 mi.

Loudon's almanac for 1787 contains another list of the stages to New Haven. Post-stages, New York to New Haven, 1787:

Harlem Heights	Hall
Kingsbridge	Shark
East Chester	Gregory
New Rochel	Williams
Marroneck	Horton
Rye	Haviland
Horseneck	Knapp
Stamford	Webb
Norwalk	Reed
Fairfield	Bulkley; Penfield; or Morehouse
Milford	Glenny
New Haven	Atwater; Smith; Miles; Larkin; or Brown

Only one name, Knapp, has survived the changes of the preceding twenty years of revolution.

It is clear, then, that travel in Colonial days was comparatively expensive and none too comfortable. It was no pleasure to take a trip in Colonial America, and so most trips were primarily of a business nature. After 1750, however, remarkable progress was made in improving the postal service and the means of transportation. The main highways developed serviceable branches into the country back of the coast, and as the nineteenth century approached, the movement westward caused new roads to be laid down west of the coastal plain.

To me it is most significant that the almanacs nowhere tell of attacks on travelers by either robbers or Indians. Civilization had not, it seems, advanced sufficiently, nor money become plentiful enough for highway robbery to be a lucrative calling, and the Indian code forbade robbing a man for gain. Indeed, Indians were surprised to find that white men took money for giving food and shelter to a traveler who was far from home. Conrad Weiser, an early traveler, tells of the scorn which Canassatego, the Onondaga chief, expressed for the hospitality of the white men:

> If a white man in travelling through our country enters one of our cabins, we treat him as I do you. We dry him, if he is wet; we warm him, if he is cold; and give him meat and drink that he may allay his hunger and thirst, and we spread soft furs for him to rest and sleep on. We demand nothing in return. But if I go into a white man's house, and ask for victuals and drink, they say, "Where is your money?" and if I have none they say, "Get out, you Indian dog."[19]

It was, indeed, the opportunity of directly discovering the Indian character from this angle that enabled some white men, as I have said, to inform their neighbors that the Indian was not merely a scalping raider, and that, even when he was, there might be a reason for his hatred. The New York almanacs contained very little about the Indians before the 1760's because of the relatively peaceful attitude of the Indians in the middle colonies. When circumstances changed this state of affairs, the typical stories of Indian cruelty and cannibalism appeared in the almanacs, but by that time a more sympathetic appraisal of the Indian side of Colonial history was being made by some traders and historians of the victorious race, and so, together with the atrocity tales, the almanacs printed accounts of Indian honesty and nobility. The Janus-faced portrait of the Indian that was drawn by the almanacs was still unchanged in the popular mind, the one representing the vengeful and cruel features of an implacable foe, the other the noble and melancholy countenance of a disinherited people.

CHAPTER 3

The Contemporary Scene

Most of the references in the almanacs to the everyday life and world of their readers are casual and incidental. We observed in the last chapter that the development of intercolonial communication was comparatively slow until about the middle of the century; there was a corresponding rate of progress in other phases of material civilization as we glimpse them through the almanacs. An idea of the general physical conditions of life at the beginning of the century is given by the *Leeds* almanac for 1700 which says that "such is the influence of this Wilderness, on the Inhabitants who are born here that it inclines them to an Indian way of living." This would imply that the foreign-born older generations of the preceding century had clung stubbornly to their European ways in so far as they were able under the conditions of the wilderness. How difficult an effort that was is illustrated by the inclusion in *Daniel Leeds,* 1694, of the "Southing of the seven Stars" so that readers might be able to calculate the time of night, since clocks and watches were very rare. In fact, eight years before, Samuel Atkins, in preparing the first Pennsylvania almanac, had given as one of the reasons for his venture the fact that the people of the province complained that they did not even know when Sunday came for lack of an almanac.[1] Almost a century later the *Hutchins* almanac for 1760 still considered it advisable to print a method of telling "by the Shadow of the moon on a sun-dial what time of night it is."

By contrast, the advertisements during the last quarter of the century indicate how great an amelioration of the material conditions of life had occurred since the beginning of the century; and while the lower classes were probably unable to enjoy most of them, it is safe to assume that some improvement took place in their lives. One could find any of the following articles in Hugh Gaine's shop at the sign of the Bible and Crown in Hanover Square: "writing paper, sealing wax and wafers, office quills and pens, pounce and pounce-boxes, pen-knives and razors, pencils, spy-glasses and pocket pistols, scales and dividers, reading glasses, leather ink-pots, red and black ink, shining sand, playing-cards, boots for the winter, Shrewsbury parchment, letter folders and sand boxes, ink powder and cake ink, pewter ink chests, violins, German flutes, fifes, battle-dores and shuttlecocks, backgammon tables, mathematical instruments, Hadley's quadrants, shaving-boxes, patent shoe blacking, pomatum, and lip-salve."[2]

The period just before and during the war with France was a time of relatively great prosperity and extravagance, and the almanacs often criticized the departure from the simple life of previous generations. The *Hutchins* almanac for 1757 expressed the hope that there would be "an Eclipse of Pride and Indecency, for which so many new Fashions arrive, and so many French Taylors and Barbers to make and promote 'em, and English Gallants such Fools as to wear 'em." Indeed, the memory of the abundance of these years during the hard years of reaction after the war added not a little fuel to the spirit of dissatisfaction which culminated in the Revolution.

Fred J. Perrine found that the American almanacs contained very little about "high living and deep drinking," and ascribed this to the fact that most of them were printed in New England. In those few instances where a convivial spirit was discovered, he declared, the effect was marred by the concluding moral.[3] The New York almanacs, however, included a good deal on the pleasures of the palate and rarely moralized about them. But most of the references appeared only after the middle of the century. From these we gather that beef and bacon were the favorite foods and beer or ale the favorite drink of the people around New York. In the *Hutchins* almanac for 1772, we read:

> Talk what you will of sallads and of capon,
> Give me a piece of good boil'd beef or bacon,
> With cabbage, or what else the world affords,
> And good strong beer, I'd not make many words.

Another almanac contained the following rapturous and patriotic alimentary ode:

> Roast Beef! belov'd by all mankind,
> If I was doom'd to have thee,
> When dress'd and garnish'd to my kind,
> And swimming in thy gravy,
> Not all thy country's force combin'd,
> Shou'd from my fury save thee . . . .
> Renown'd Sir Loin, ofttimes decreed
> The theme of English ballad,
> E'en Kings on thee have joy'd to feed,
> Unknown to Frenchman's palate.

> O how much doth thy taste exceed
> Soup meagre, frogs, and sallad.[4]

The popular attitude toward water as a thirst quencher is revealed in these verses:

> You'd think him mad, or near the Matter,
> Who Ale forsakes to drink *cold Water!*
> Except Necessity require
> Water, to quench a Fever's Fire.[5]

The reader was also advised:

> To cheer thy Heart, and make thee merry,
> Drink now and then a Cup of Sherry;
> Tho' (I do think that) Beer's as good
> To warm both Heart and also Blood.[6]

Tea was introduced into the colonies in the early part of the century and soon was the butt of attack in newspapers and almanacs as a foolish and vain extravagance. It seems that many colonists were in the beginning unfamiliar with the method of preparing it, for we hear of some who, after boiling the tea leaves in water for a time, threw the water away and ate the leaves. Those who did not find the leaves to their taste tried to improve the taste by adding butter and salt.[7]

The *Hutchins* almanac for 1763 contained a humorous "Receipt for an Asthma," which incidentally gives one a bird's-eye view of some of the popular foods and drinks of the time. The author of the effusion gave advice to his asthmatic friend, Marcus, about what edibles and potables he must avoid or eat to stay comfortably alive. Among those to be shunned, he mentioned: meats preserved in salt, liquors made of malt, "season'd sauce," hams, tongues, "pidgeon pies"; and

> If ven'son pasty's set before ye,
> Each bit you eat, "memento mori."

However, Marcus need not starve himself, for he was allowed at one meal:

> A neck, a loin, or leg of veal.
> Young turkeys I allow you four,
> Partridges, pullets half a score.
> Of house-lamb boil'd, eat quarters two.
> The devil's in't if that won't do.
> Now, as to liquor, why indeed . . .
> Glasses of wine t'extinguish drought,
> Drink two with water, three without.

In the *Rivington* almanac for 1774 on the February calendar page, the reader was also reminded that:

> Pancakes and fritters now in season are,
> And young men they for Valentines prepare.

Another almanac poem sang the praises not only of beef and bacon but of "ruddy Peaches," "plump figs," "long-keeping Russets," "Cath'rine Pears," "Pearmains" (a French variety of apple), "Codlings," (cooking apples), "wheaten Plumbs," "black Damsons," "Coleworts," beans, "Plumb-Pudding," "sweet spic'd cake," and apple pies.[8] There is an allusion to a popular dish of the eighteenth century in this rhyme: "Now Doll, the dairy-maid, will club With Roger for a *sillabub.*" This delicacy was generally made by curdling milk or cream with wine or cider, and then sweetening and flavoring it. For cold mornings, *Hutchins,* 1774 recommended "Cherry Bounce" and toast. So we see that the colonists had plenty of good things to eat and drink to compensate them in part for the lack of material conveniences.

The rigors of the wilderness did not seem to affect woman's impulse to be as young and beautiful as nature and art can make her. The impulse was reflected in such proverbs as "Time makes wrinkles in spite of the Leaden Fore-head-Cloath";[9] and it is revealed in the beauty preparations advertised by the printer and the favorite recipes of readers which the almanac-authors passed along. "The Princely beautifying Lotion" sold by Hugh Gaine was guaranteed to remove the pits of smallpox and the wrinkles of time and trouble and to make the haggard and old "look young, beautiful and fair."[10] Those who could not afford to buy a bottle might try the lemon-and-milk preparation which a kind reader had found very efficacious in beautifying her face.[11] Lemon and milk are popular folk lotions. The almanacs, however, are silent respecting the beauty of New York women in general. Perhaps the reason is implied in a surprising comparison of the women of New York with those of Boston which the observant Dr. Alexander Hamilton made in 1744. He says:

> I must take notice that this place [Boston] abounds with pretty women, who appear rather more abroad than they do at York, and dress elegantly. They are for the most part free and affable as well as pretty. I saw not one prude while I was there.[12]

Complaints first began to appear in the almanacs after 1750 regarding the custom of the dowry and settlement. Parents protested that their hair was turning gray and their families were being impoverished on account of "the fear to be overburthened with daughters, because one cannot be rid of them, nor drive them away but with a rod of silver."[13] Marriageable young men also criticized the unreasonable settlements demanded by parents for daughters with rich portions.[14] The common people were not much upset by this problem, it seems, for we read in the *Rivington* almanac for 1775 that the average age of marriage for both sexes was approximately twenty, and that it was relatively easy for a young man to support a family.

In this connection let us consider the proportion of females to males in the population figures published in the almanacs. For example, a census of Burlington, Monmouth, Essex, and Middlesex counties in New Jersey made at the beginning of the century cited about nine white females to ten white males.[15] On the other hand, the census of New York City in June, 1756 showed about thirteen females to ten males,[16] but this proportion was not typical of the province as a whole, for the census of the state published in the *Father Hutchins* almanac for 1792 indicated about nine females to ten males, the ratio that had existed at the beginning of the century.

The population statistics given in the almanacs tell of very rapid growth, which, to be truly appreciated, must be compared with the figures on the expectation of life in that century. The *Titan Leeds* almanac for 1725 contained a computation by "Capt. Haily of Oxford," who stated that of every 1,000 born, 360 died before the age of six; 600 before sixteen; 840 before twenty-six; and 900 before forty-six. The *Greenleaf* almanac for 1793, while it showed an improvement, still disclosed a very high mortality rate. According to this table, 460 of every 1000 died before ten; 504 before twenty; and 615 before forty. Compare these figures with the corresponding vital statistics for the United States in 1975; 21 of every 1000 died before ten; 28 before twenty; and 59 before forty.[17]

In spite of this great increase in population in the eighteenth century, New York and Albany were the only large towns in the province. New York had tripled its population from about 10,000 in 1756 to about 30,000 in 1775, and Albany claimed 3,600 inhabitants in 1775. The other towns were hardly more than villages.[18] The *New York Pocket Almanac* for 1771 includes an interesting "Prospect of the City of New York" opposite the title page. In the foreground one sees ships at anchor in the East River; in the background Manhattan Island, covered with houses, churches, public buildings, farmsteads, and trees.

The trees must have been a very pleasant feature of the streets in those days; they attracted the attention of the noted traveler Peter Kalm when he visited New York in 1748–1749, which because of them "seemed quite like a garden."

Crossing the East River to Brooklyn or the bay to Staten Island at that time involved considerable risk, owing to the strong tides and currents and the squalls of wind for which the harbor has always been known. Capsizings and other accidents occurred not infrequently. For instance, in urging the legislature to equip the ferry boats to Staten Island with the cork waistcoats invented by Dubourg, *Roger More* remarked in 1764: "If this had been done before, the late Loss of the Lives of 8 valuable Persons from this Place would have been prevented."

The key below the "Prospect" refers to the following landmarks going north, that is, from left to right from the Battery: Fort George, with a British flag over it; the Jews' Synagogue; the Old Dutch Church; the Lutheran Church; Trinity Church; Presbyterian Meeting House; the New Scots' Meeting House; the North Dutch Church; the Quaker Meeting House; the Calvinist Church; the Anabaptist Meeting House; the Methodist Meeting House; the Moravian Meeting House; the North Dutch Calvinist Church; St. Paul's Church; St. George's Chapel; King's College (now Columbia College); the New Brick Meeting House; the North Lutheran Church; the Prison. It will be observed that only two of these buildings were of a purely secular character, the fort and the jail. A list of public buildings in a pocket almanac for 1766 contains the names of several not included in the "Prospect": the City Hall (and public library); the Alms House; the Exchange; the old Hospital at the Battery; the Barracks; and the Markets. This old Hospital was established in 1699 and is not to be confused with the New York Hospital, which was charted June 13, 1771 and opened for patients in 1791.

The markets occupied a prominent place in the public mind at this time because of a law regulating prices in them, abstracts of which were printed in the almanacs for 1764.[19] The law had been passed toward the end of the war with France to check profiteering in food products, which had raised prices so high that they had become "not only ruinous to Families of the poorer Sort, but intolerable even to People of better Estate." I quote some of the maximum prices fixed by the law, that they may be compared with present prices, but it must be remembered that they were well above the average for that period:

Beef . . . . .7–9 cents a lb.
Pork . . . . .8–10 cents a lb.
Veal . . . . .10–12 cents a lb.
Mutton . . . . .7–9 cents a lb.
Lamb . . . . .8–18 cents a lb.
Butter . . . . .18–30 cents a lb.
Milk . . . . .4–5 cents a qt.

An important provision of the law was that hucksters and retailers were forbidden to buy in the markets before noon, since the markets were primarily intended for the use of housekeepers. A vivid description of a morning in these markets has come down to us in a letter written by a lady in the year the law was passed, who wrote:

> I have frequently observed, and sometimes felt, great
> rudeness and ill manners in our public markets
> . . . sometimes the prey has been seized and in danger
> of being torn to pieces by two furious combatants,
> equally voracious, who seemed by their actions to be
> upon the point of starving and to contend for their lives.
> I, who am a woman unused to war and of a peaceable
> disposition, have been obliged to give up my pretensions
> to the goods, half-purchased, and give place to one of
> more strength and resolution, being not quite reduced to
> the necessity of fighting or starving. . . . Such conduct
> has also a direct tendency to raise the price of provisions
> in the market to the extravagant price that we all have
> had reason to complain of.[20]

Lists of public buildings in the almanacs failed to mention one
which was used by the public more than any of those named—the
tavern. Conditions had caused the Colonial taverns to develop during
the second half of the eighteenth century into a unique institution
whose varied functions are fully appreciated only if it is realized that
they not only were used as restaurants and hotels but also often performed services which today are dispensed by gambling houses,
clubhouses, community houses, post offices, gasoline stations, rail-
road and bus terminals, local newspapers, circuses, legislative and
judicial chambers, libraries, evening schools, museums, concert halls,
and theaters. People came there to talk over business or political deals
as they ate and drank, to meet a traveler from a distant place or read
the latest newspaper, to attend meetings of the merchants' exchange,
chamber of commerce, or legislature, to improve their skill in reading,
writing, and spelling,[21] to listen to a concert, see an extraordinary
exhibition, or hear a forbidden play shrewdly disguised to escape the
law, like *Othello,* for example, which was advertised as "a series of
Moral Dialogues in Five Parts depicting the evil effects of jealousy and
other bad passions and Proving that happiness can only spring from
the pursuit of Virtue."[22]

One of Benjamin Franklin's friends once said: "I have heard Dr.
Franklin relate with great pleasantry that in travelling when he was
young, the first step he took for his tranquillity and to obtain immediate attention at the inns, was to anticipate inquiry by saying, 'My
name is Benjamin Franklin. I was born in Boston. I am a printer by
profession, am travelling to Philadelphia, shall have to return at such
a time, and have no news. Now, what can you give me for dinner?' "[23]

The New York almanacs refer mainly to the taverns as places of
social resort and post-stages. The *Clapp* almanac for 1699, for example,
had this note on the June calendar page:

The 24 of this month is celebrated the Feast of St. John Baptist, in commemoration of which (& to keep up a happy union of lasting friendship by the sweet harmony of good society) a feast is held by the Johns of this City, at John Clapps in the Bowry, where any Gentleman whose Christian name is John may find a hearty wellcome to join in comfort with his Namesakes.

Two of the best known taverns in New York were Cape's and Fraunce's, both of which were prominent in the business and social life of the city before and after the Revolution. Cape's Tavern had been known before the Revolution as the Province Arms. It had been built by Etienne De Lancey about 1700 and had been the residence of James De Lancey in the early part of the century. John Cape, who had been a lieutenant in the Continental Army, secured control of it after the evacuation of the city by the British. Being a Freemason and a member of the Society of Cincinnati helped him to make it the scene of many important events of the period such as Washington's reply to the welcoming address of the citizens of New York in 1783 and the dinner of Governor Clinton to the French ambassador in the same year. In February, 1786, however, Cape suddenly disappeared, to the regret of his creditors. In 1792 the old building was torn down and replaced by the City Hotel, which attained great prominence in the early part of the next century. We have noticed among the names of proprietors of taverns on the post-roads to Albany the Widow Vernon's in Albany and the Widow Van Allen's on the east side of the Hudson River, about twenty-seven miles south of Albany—evidence of the fact that tavern-keeping was often the resort of widows of small means, some of whom were quite successful.

There was another side of the taverns that should not be overlooked. This aspect is illustrated by a terse "Description of a Tavern," which is found in the *Hutchins* almanac for 1783:

Thither Libertines repair to drink away their brains and p—— away their estates . . . . Thither Young Quality retire to spend their tradesmen's money, and to delight themselves with the impudence of lewd harlots . . . whilst their Ladies . . . are glad to break a commandment with their own footmen. . . . Thither run Sots . . . that they may either wash away the reflections of their own past follies or forget the treachery of their friends, the falsehood of their wives, the disobedience of their children, the roguery of their lawyers, . . . or the ingratitude of the world . . . .

The tavern, as I have said, was the meeting place of clubs and

However, the only satisfactory approach to the language of the common people is indirect—through the pages of the almanacs themselves. Nothing can quite take the place of reading a substantial number of these old annuals from cover to cover. The present-day reader will find the style unpolished but vigorous, its main characteristic being an apparent indifference to rules, whether of grammar or sentence structure or verbal propriety. As he bumps along over an interminable sentence, the frequent stops at commas and semicolons on the way to the haven of the period will be welcomed. He will also probably relish the vernacular words for the primary bodily functions that were dropped casually by many almanac-authors as if they were ignorant or disdainful of the prophylactic Latin equivalents. And he will enjoy the concrete, familiar imagery of the proverbs: "Love and the cough cannot be hid,"[29] "Eternity hath no grey hairs."[30] He will be delighted, too, by the Elizabethan exuberance which can be sampled in this selection from the *Hutchins* almanac for 1770:

> Now the Spring approaches, many of your amber-grease gallants, as brave Gentlemen as the tailor can make them, shall go a wooing to rich heiresses, being strongly provided with honey words, sugar-candy expressions, and most delicious sentences; being likewise not without store of stewed anagrams, baked epigrams, soused madrigals, pickled roundelays, broiled sonnets, and parboiled elegies.

In general, the unfamiliar turns of expression, phrases, and words will add an antique charm to the reading, as, for example: "We are like to have,"[31] "Merchants traffic to foreign nations,"[32] "sottish Chouse" [dupe];[33] "span new,"[34] "hab nab at a Venture,"[35] "Blood warm suds,"[36] "Sparagrass."[37]

In retrospect, the war with France marked a turning point in the development of Colonial America, as did the First World War in the history of the United States. Both conflicts came at the end of a period of growth in material and cultural resources—a time of harvest for the colonies after the settlement of the wilderness and for the United States after the physical and economic subjugation of the continent. In both instances the harvest-time was followed by a wintry season of hardship, disillusion, turbulence, and redirection.

This chapter has been concerned with some of the fruits of the harvest season, the rapid improvement in material resources and conditions of living around the middle of the century. The Colonial almanacs bear witness to this change and growth, but in a disjointed fashion. The picture must be pieced together from many scattered items: a poem in praise of beef, an advertisement of beauty preparations, vital statistics, an engraving, the digest of a law regulating the markets, a list of public buildings and private societies, a notice in a tavern, and the like, but as the pieces are put together, the imagination sees a land beginning at last to smile upon its conquerors, whose character, after a long apprenticeship in the hard, free life of the New World, had become plain, tough, unconventional, and independent.

CHAPTER 4

Opinion and Prejudice

Certain popular beliefs and prejudices reflected in the New York almanacs seem to have maintained a flourishing existence throughout the period of this study. I have grouped them for convenience under four heads: the medical and legal professions, money, women, and the ideal of the happy life. To judge by the space devoted to these topics, they were a never-failing source of interest to the readers of the almanacs.

Medicine and the Law

We know that the power and prestige of lawyers and doctors increased greatly during the eighteenth century, but the almanacs show that the popular attitude toward them, based upon centuries of previous experience of their ignorance and unscrupulousness, remained unaltered. There was at that time, moreover, sufficient ground in fact for the distrust and dislike of the people. The education and regulation of these professions was still in a lamentably primitive state. There were few well-educated doctors or lawyers in the colonies before the Revolution. A man could become a physician in New York in 1757 without taking an examination or getting a license and could treat patients without the least fear of punishment for malpractice.[1] Quacks naturally abounded "like Locusts in Egypt."[2] In New England, conditions were no better. The *Ames* almanac for 1765 remarked that, since the war with France, "many idle Persons, . . . finding they must get a Living some how or other, and having but poor Stomachs to return to the Stall or Plough, from whence they came; some of them commence Quacks, and call themselves Doctors, having seen a Man that saw another Man cured of a very foul Gunshot by hot Oil of Turpentine, and heard their Grandmother say that

Carduus Tea will vomit—thus . . . they become famous Water Gruel Doctors."[3] And the condition of the legal profession was probably the same, or worse.

In the popular mind the two professions were constantly associated. The grievance behind a rhyme like

> Thus Sickness bringeth to Physician's Health
> And so our Folly gives the Lawyer's Wealth[4]

was frequently expressed and was echoed in other sources. An early historian, Gabriel Thomas, in describing the Quaker settlements in Pennsylvania and western New Jersey, wrote in 1698:

> Of lawyers and physicians I shall say nothing, because the country is very peaceable and healthy; long may it continue so and never have occasion for the tongue of the one and the pen of the other, both equally destructive to men's estates and lives; besides, forsooth, they, hangman-like, have a license to murder and make mischief.[5]

The popular view regarding doctors seems to have been founded on the deep conviction that they were ignorant but concealed the fact to some extent by using a mysterious professional jargon:

> A physician it is observed, is a grave formal animal who picks our pockets by calling unintelligible fluff in a sick man's chamber till nature cures or medicine kills him.[6]

The number of avoidable fatalities must have been very great, and people believed that it was very often more exact to say after the death of a patient not "that he died of a fever or a pleurisy, but that he died of the Doctor."[7] Some of the most bitter comments will be found on the March calendar pages, since that was the busiest month for the medicos: "This Month physicians have hardly time to say their prayers, they are so employ'd in killing sick people."[8] Accordingly, the almanac-author advised his reader to put his trust in nature, a much safer and less expensive physician, and in those cases where nature's aid was not enough, to avail himself of well-established popular remedies like those printed in his almanac.

Lawyers were castigated even more frequently than doctors. Indeed, it is very hard to find a Colonial almanac of the eighteenth century without at least one slap at the legal profession. If there was no space on the other pages, the page of court sessions usually made room for an insulting rhyme. Undoubtedly, one reason for making them a target so often was the inclination of the colonists to rush into lawsuits in spite of the general belief in the dishonesty of lawyers. This was the common charge brought against them, that it was unprofitable for lawyers to settle disputes; hence they did what they could to create them, and there was no hope of peace in a community as long as it harbored a lawyer. There was nothing nobler than an honest lawyer, but

> Shall we such Lawyers see, till the Loud Trump
> 'Wakes all, in Sleeping Ashes, from the Dump?[9]

The resentment of the people, however, was not confined to the subject of the dishonesty of lawyers. It went much further and deeper and was directed against the weaknesses of the legal system itself. The perversion of justice through venality of judges was frequently noted. A good example is a poem entitled "The Law-Suit," which deals with the bribing of the judge by both sides. The plaintiff gave him a coach, the defendant a pair of horses. When the decision was announced in favor of the latter, the plaintiff exclaimed: "O Coach, . . . thou art the wrong way gone!" But the judge blandly replied:

> . . . It cannot but be so;
> For where his Horses draw, your Coach must go![10]

By contrast, the Oriental method of securing incorruptible judges was presented in a tale illustrating the wisdom of Cambyses, king of Persia. Upon learning of a lapse on the part of one of his judges, he ordered the offender to be put to death and then flayed, and afterward appointed the dead judge's son to the vacant place. To make sure that the mistake would not be repeated, he furthermore commanded that the dead father's skin be hung above the seat of justice, where the son could always see it upon entering the court.[11]

Experience showed, however, that knavish lawyers and purchasable judges were not the only evils of the law. The delays incident to legal procedure and the expensiveness of legal service interfered no less with the proper administration of justice. For these reasons, the remedy of the law was worse than the disease, even when the integrity of counsel and court was unimpeachable. Lawsuits ate up so much money that victory was no better than defeat. The situation was summed up in the *Hutchins* almanac for 1753 by the story of two beggars who found an oyster and could not come to an agreement about the right of ownership. Being civilized beggars, however, they selected a judge to settle the dispute, and he, after due deliberation, ate the oyster, and, in all fairness, gave each of them a shell. Sometimes the criticism of the dilatoriness of judicial procedure used the weapon of ridicule, as in the summary of a case which the author claimed was taken from English legal history. At a country assize one of the jurymen asked the judge for permission to step out of the court for a moment. The request was unusual, and so the judge embarked on an examination of precedents while the poor man waited impatiently. Old yearbooks, the principle of *nisi prius,* Lord Coke, and other authorities were carefully consulted, until, at last, the juryman, unable to contain himself any longer, informed the judge that he withdrew his previous request, the original necessity having passed. Unfortunately, the juryman was a poor man and had borrowed the breeches. He could neither replace them in their original condition nor pay for them, and was sued. The result was that he and his family were ruined.[12]

Another feature of the legal system that aroused dissatisfaction was the jury, the objection to which is put succinctly by *Thomas More* (1752), who said that it might be better to submit a dispute "to the Arbitration of two or three wise men, rather than leave it to the Decision of one knave and eleven Fools." However, no method of selecting the wise men was proposed.

Finally, we must note here that there was some recognition during the century of a certain very grave defect in the administration of justice, although it was not often referred to: the fact that the scales of justice are weighted in favor of the rich and influential. The almanacs do not protest strongly against this fundamental flaw, but they nevertheless raised the question:

> Why should the Law a Cobweb be,
> Small Flies to catch while great go free?[13]

Money

Inasmuch as money has always occupied a very important place in the thoughts of men, and was, besides, an article of great scarcity in Colonial America, the views that were often expressed in the almanacs regarding it are of interest. In general, its usefulness was not underestimated. The colonists were well aware that the possession of it gave freedom and independence and power, and they regarded the loss of it as a tragedy of the first magnitude.[14] They were constantly reminded of the urgency of accumulating it, and they did not seem to have idealized the absence of it. When they thought of poverty, they hated it, and were determined to avoid it by every means in their power. The versifier who cried:

> O Poverty! thou nauseous, bitter Pill!
> Thou strong Provocative to all that's ill!
> Thou Bane of Love, and Happiness of Life,
> Parent of Woe, and of domestic Strife![15]

was echoing their sentiments. On the other hand, they did not believe that it was good to hoard money like a miser, or to have too much of it. Only the man of moderate wealth, in their opinion, enjoyed the benefits of money without the evils attendant on a deficiency or excess of it.

At the same time, they had inherited the ancient tradition that money was the source of this world's evil, and the almanacs contain many items like the following:

> In Saturn's Reign, when Money was unfound,
> Then was that Age with Peace and Plenty Crown'd;
> Then Mine was Thine, Thine Mine, and all our Lives
> All things in common were, except our Wives;
> Now, he whom Love of Money Doth beset,
> For's own Soul, or's Wives Body much cares not.[16]

> Money makes the physician promise you health when you are dying; puts an ignoramus into office; makes the lawyer set a good face upon an ill matter; hides some time a *Non Con Tubster* [dissenting preacher] under a gown and cassoc, and persuades him to conform, reform, deform and submit to any form, for the sake of his Goddess Pecunia.[17]

Women

The subject of the fair sex was a prime favorite of the New York almanacs, and, as one might expect, was treated almost entirely from the man's point of view. At its best, his attitude was essentially possessive and patronizing, and his manner that of a good master talking about a troublesome but indispensable and charming servant. Most women probably accepted the relationship unquestioningly and only hoped that the master would exercise his prerogative with gentle sway. For example, a young woman, giving advice in verse to young wives, counseled a spirit of subservience such as no man of the time could find fault with.[18] There could be no doubt that she agreed with the saying:

> . . . Man has Title to the upper Hand,
> A Woman may ask, but Man should command.[19]

The first requirement of the Master in considering a womanservant for a life position was termed "virtue." This, apparently, was not an easy thing for women to retain. Certain men were so bad and women were so weak that only unceasing vigilance could save their "virtue" from an early demise. They were advised to

> . . . avoid with Care
> All close Engagements in Love's fatal War
> Tho' long uninjured you maintain the Fight,
> You'll find your only Safety's in your Flight.[20]

In brief:

> Woman, like Glass, is frail and weak,
> As apt to slide, as apt to break.
> Guard, therefore, every step with Caution;
> For just as Glass . . . is Reputation:
> Both broke to Pieces at one falling,
> For ever lost and past recalling.[21]

And therefore: "He comes too near, that comes to be deny'd."[22]

"The Terrible Consequences of a Young Woman's losing her Virtue" is the title of one of many selections on that theme. It is the story

> of one Abah Rabieh at Aleppo, whose only Daughter having stain'd the Honour of his Family, by a criminal Amour, he killed her with his own Hands, and having invited all his Relations to dine with him, in the Midst of the Entertainment, caus'd her Head to be set before them in a Dish, swimming in its Blood.[23]

The next day he "retired . . . into the Deserts of Arabia." Under those circumstances, it is no wonder that people thought at that time that a "Man and a Woman that can be together alone, and yet preserve chastity, can break no law."[24]

Reformed rakes were no less insistent on the point of woman's virtue. After years spent in error and sin, they would suddenly see that they had taken the wrong road to felicity. Repentant, they married a virtuous girl and found that this was the only happiness and peace.[25] But no one dreamed of extending the same privilege of experimentation to both sexes, or of demanding that men who had made a mistake should have their choice limited to women who had made the same mistake.

New fashions for women usually stirred up a hue and cry over the virtue of those who first dared to follow them. The hoopskirt, which nowadays expresses olden grace and innocence, was in the beginning labeled a "Whores Invention,"[26] and the women who wore them were accused of having the devil as their only guide. The *Jacob Taylor* almanac for 1726, printed by Sam. Keimer in Philadelphia, contained this couplet:

Now Madam with French Fashions must be fooling,
And wear a Hoop as if their Tails want cooling.

A fashion popular during the war with France was disapproved in these terms:

> I hope my Female Readers won't be offended, if I tell 'em that a Castle secured only by Flankers, and the Front and Rear left in a Manner Defenceless, is in great danger (if in earnest besieged) of being soon stormed and all the Treasure taken.[27]

Fashions that had survived the initial hostility to them remained to offer an inexhaustible source of masculine banter, the burden of which was that women would be more attractive without these artificial aids. Those prose or verse pieces ridiculing contemporary fashions must have pleased not only the male readers of the almanacs but also the poor female readers who longed for a glimpse of the world of fashion. The hoop continued to be the butt of ridicule until the end of the century. For instance, a humorous poem on the "Origin of Hoops" in the *Loudon* almanac for 1787 says that Dame Fashion, finding that the elaborate headdress of the time made women top-heavy, decided to restore their equilibrium, and "onerate the bottom."

Having assured himself of the virtue of a candidate for the honor of running his household, the Master next turned his attention to certain other qualifications. The second question that he probably asked himself was, "Has she any money?" While this does not seem to have been a prerequisite to matrimony in Colonial America, it certainly was an important consideration to very many men, who followed the advice of the one who wrote:

> If you are proffered a wife with only one of these three properties, beauty, wit, wealth, choose the last, for these are compared to a walnut: Beauty is like the rind, quickly peeled off; wit like the shell, quickly cracked; but wealth, like the kernel, brings substance along with it.[28]

There are many instances in the New York almanacs of women being advised to marry a man even if he was poor,[29] but none that I remember urging the reverse, except a brief account of the opinions of William Penn on marriage in the *Hutchins* almanac for 1772.

Beauty was generally regarded as a dangerous thing in a wife, and worth risking only where all the desirable characteristics were also present. This placed beauty at an almost insuperable disadvantage. It was more important that the prospective bride should be good-natured and should have an aversion to "Plays or public Shows,"[30] or that she should be "neither a Foe, nor Slave to Love," and sensibly religious.[31] Her sense of economy was also a serious consideration, of which an amusing test is offered in a poem entitled, "The Choice of a Wife by Cheese."[32] This was used by a young man who could not quite make up his mind as to which of three sisters he should marry. He finally hit on the idea of asking each of them to cut up a cheese. The first, to show how economical she would be, ate the paring; the second, to show how generous she would be, threw away the rind; and the third, a happy medium, scraped off the cheese, and carried it off in triumph. A set of qualifications which appeared several times covered some of the minor requirements. These demanded that the future wife should be "Young by all Means," have "no Learning . . . either ancient or modern upon any Consideration whatever," excepting a sufficient skill in English, show "in Spelling a little becoming Deficiency," be in "the Doctrine of Punctuation (or what is generally called 'Stopping') by no means conversant," and finally, stay not "always in the Parlour, but sometimes in the Kitchen."[33]

What a man expected of his wife after marriage was set forth metrically in *Hutchins*, 1765, by a young woman, who declared that the province of a wife was small and her sphere in life narrow. It should be her delight to act properly within that limited area and make her husband bless the day when he gave his liberty away. The education of his children and the care of his household were her chief duties. She must be frugal and clean. Her person should be always neat, for "If once fair decency is fled, Love soon deserts the genial bed." The most dangerous period of marriage was the first few years. It must be her "peculiar care" to see that disaster was averted during that period. She could help by a "kind obliging carriage" and by "dressing her mind" to charm his reason. She should always meet him with a smile, and avoid storms by never engaging "in wordy war." She must never match his rage with her own and never criticize his good sense, a thing which few husbands forgave. When he was troubled with care, she must sympathize and claim her "share of pain." In a word,

> From rising morn till setting night
> To see him pleas'd your chief delight.

In return it was his duty, whether his wife was sick or well, to love and cherish her, "even tho' she may not altogether answer his most Sanguine Expectations."[34]

American men were warned against giving their wives any power, the disastrous example of Englishmen in this matter being set before them.[35] The henpecked husband mated to a scolding shrew, in particular, was a situation that received a great deal of attention in the

New York almanacs,[36] and the past as well as the present was drawn upon for illustration. The case of Socrates and Xantippe was introduced to show how old the evil was. In "The Medicine. A Tale for the Ladies," a remedy was suggested.[37] John had married Molly, fair, young, and the toast of the town, but shrewish. Before long he began to find excuses to go out evenings. Desperate, she consulted a wise old uncle who told her that he had an elixir that was guaranteed to cure quarrels between husbands and wives. This she was to take a few spoonfuls of whenever a dispute was on the verge of breaking out, and keep the liquid in her mouth for several minutes, smiling and looking pleased the while. She was to use it for a month. It worked wonders, although, as she learned later, it was merely water. A reconciliation was quickly effected, and peace and love reigned between them. This story recalls an unusual feature in the *New Jersey Almanack* for 1770, a series of questions and answers on general matters, science, and religion, the first category including advice remarkably similar to the stuff put out by modern purveyors of "advice to the lovelorn." I quote two examples:

> Q. I am troubled by desire. What shall I do?
> A. Meditate "on the Realms above," and get married.
> Q. I am a Widow. I am wildly courted. His two maiden sisters hate me. What shall I do?
> A. Marry him.

The Happy Life

What do the almanacs suggest that their readers regarded as the happy life? Generally, they show that he dreamed of a life of independence and moderate enjoyment, untouched by the restless fever of greed or ambition. In the early part of the century, a typical representation of the happy life would include these elements: honest dealings and friendly relations with one's neighbors, avoidance of the oppression and exploitation suffered by the poor, faithful observance of the monogamic code, and wholehearted service to God.[38]

When we come to the period before the Revolution, we note that there was greater emphasis on the material and cultural pleasures of life. The *Hutchins* almanac for 1771 and the *Freeman* almanac for 1772 offer examples that are almost identical. We know that the author of the *Freeman* almanac was a leader of the Sons of Liberty in New York and wrote from the point of view of those who were soon to support the Revolution. In his almanac the imaginary home of the happy man was called "Freeman's-Hill." Let us see what the *Freeman* ideal was. Looking toward Freeman's-Hill, we first observe a "pretty little country seat," behind which there is a charming little garden and a little orchard rich in fruits. Nearby a sparkling "little rill" flows along musically. The house is surrounded by woodland good for hunting. In the cellar a "little store of wine" of old vintage is always to be found. The library upstairs contains the "best authors, new and old," and on the floor near the most comfortable chair lies the master's pipe. Occasionally, he fills an idle hour listening to good music. He has one or two real friends, and, best of all, "a pretty little spouse." Standing beside her, he utters this final wish:

> Be the produce of our joys
> Little girls and little boys.

Freeman's ideal, with one critical exception, followed in most respects the literary tradition best expressed in John Pomfret's poem, "The Choice," which was enormously popular at that time. Pomfret's dreamer is a bachelor who prefers the occasional companionship of "some obliging modest fair" to daily association with a pretty little spouse and little girls and boys. However, a social reformer like Freeman could not very well recommend a way of life that did not provide for the propagation of more freemen.

Twenty years later, the ideal was essentially unchanged,[39] the only new element being the wish to be free from "the bitter Rage of Party Zeal," which the task of building a new nation had engendered to shatter the quiet of Freeman's-Hill. Even if his dream was not yet a reality after the sacrifice of revolution, it did not seem so far away.

CHAPTER 5

Almanac Humor

It has been observed by many that the Colonial almanac of the eighteenth century was the father of American humor.[1] It would perhaps be more accurate to say that the father is not known for certain, as sometimes happens, but that the prime suspect is the almanac. During the eighteenth century, the almanac was the sole source of humorous writing to which the common people of America had continuous access, from year to year. This is a fact significant in itself, but it takes on greater weight if we recall that humorous writing outside the almanacs was almost nonexistent in the seventeenth century and generally undistinguished and intermittent during the next century. Consequently, the impress of the humor of the almanacs was deepened not only by its extensive circulation and continuous activity but also by lack of competition and the inchoate state of American humor before the nineteenth century. The popular kind of humor developed by the almanacs during the preceding century gained an ascendancy which has not yet been quite relinquished, and the success of the popular style and matter used by *Daniel Leeds, Nathaniel Ames,* and *Poor Richard* has exercised a tremendous influence on the main line of American humorists, from the *Jack Downing* of Jackson's day to Will Rogers. These almanac-authors were undeniably the first to give shape to that humorous American folk character dubbed by Jennette Tandy "Uncle Sam, the unlettered philosopher,"[2] who, under various incarnations, has represented the spirit of native American humor in each new generation since the beginning of the nineteenth century—self-educated, warmhearted, wise old democrat and freewheeling, irreverent commentator on the American scene.

Following the example of *Daniel Leeds,* the New York almanacs offered their readers a type of humor apparently suited to their tastes and interests—rustic, coarse, often caustic, and sometimes unprintable, except by present-day standards. The last-named characteristic, however, is not to be construed to imply that the almanacs slipped now and then into pornography. Nothing could be further from the truth. The references are so free from salacious self-consciousness that it is more just to regard them as indications of a rural attitude toward sex based on intimate contact with nature.[3] The catering to the rural reader may also be observed in the large number of humorous items on the weather, the seasons, city "dudes" and "slickers," and tradesmen, and in the numerous instances of a straight-faced, tongue-in-cheek humor, still dear to the American farmer.

Occasionally, the prevailing lack of refinement lapsed into painfully bad taste. For instance, a piece of verse in the *Hutchins* almanac for 1776 represented a husband commenting on the inscription above his wife's grave in these words:

> Sleep on—I've got another wife
> And therefore cannot come to thee,
> For I must go to bed to she.

Then there was the instance in the *Hutchins* almanac for 1763 of "Sir Marmaduke Wyvill's" reaction in meter to the news of the approximately simultaneous deaths of his horse, his mistress, and his wife:

> I've lost my Mistress, Horse, and Wife;
> But when I think on human Life,
> I'm glad it is no worse.
> My wife was ugly, and a Scold;
> My Mistress was grown lean and old;
> I'm sorry for my Horse.

But the *New York and Country Almanack* for 1776 liked it well enough to appropriate it.

The astrological features of the almanac gave rise to a dry sort of humor that would please everybody without offending the superstitious and incidentally enabled the usually skeptical almanac-author to let off steam safely. Suppose, as often happened, he was deluged with complaints about the accuracy of his weather predictions. The *Leeds* almanacs had shown the way out early in the century, as expressed in this couplet from the *Titan Leeds* almanac for 1721:

> When we tell of the weather, we
> Tell not in what Country such will be.

But there were many variations on the theme, of which I shall mention two typical examples. Two wine experts came to a disagreement over a certain hogshead of wine. One of them, having tasted the wine, said that it had the flavor of iron; the other, who had smelled it, thought it smacked of leather. The difference of opinion between the experts did not, it seems, interfere with the consumption of the wine, for the hogshead was empty in a few days, and then they found at the bottom an iron key with a goat's-leather thong attached to it; therewith the author remarked: "so we say, it will rain or it will snow &c but we cannot tell exactly where't will fall."[4] A further development of this type is the story of the pastor who finally had the courage and sense to accept a position which had remained unoccupied for a long time because the parishioners insisted that the candidate first promise to oblige them with whatever weather they wanted. He agreed to the condition, was appointed, and within a few days called a meeting. He announced at the meeting that he was prepared to fulfill his promise, but he must first know what kind his parishioners wanted. Of course, they could not come to an agreement, since not everyone finds the same weather convenient or profitable. Their folly was tactfully exposed, and the pastor had a job for life.[5] There was also humorous intent as well as slyness in the customary method of arranging the weather predictions, which were so strung out down the column on the calendar page that any one of the words covered three or four days.

The humor of unexpected juxtapositions of words and sayings in the same column probably was not always accidental, as, for example, the adjacency of the entry for the anniversary of King George III's coronation (*Hutchins, 1767*, September 22) and the adage: "a Fool and a Fidler are much alike both delighting in noise." The preface to *Wing Reviv'd* for 1762 shows that almanac-authors sometimes, at least, were fond of this kind of innuendo, incidentally a device very popular in the later history of American humor:

> In the Column of remarkable Days, I have placed both Saints and Sinners, not knowing the particular Time of all their Deaths or Births, so must leave them, or you, to make a Separation.

The pages devoted to the eclipses of the year often contained humorous "prognostications" ridiculing the proverbial cautiousness of astrologers. A good example is the paragraph on the page of eclipses in the *Hutchins* almanac for 1756, which predicted:

> An "Eclipse of Honesty" among "Men and Ladies of Pleasure,"

> An "Eclipse of Money" among "Poets, Star-gazers, and would-be Merchants,"

> An "Eclipse of Modesty" among "those young Ladies that go naked breasted and broad-sterned,"

An "Eclipse of Truth" among shopkeepers, and

"An "Eclipse of Beauty," which "will be very dark and visible in the Faces of old Bawds, common Strumpets, and Scolding Wives."

Finally it predicted that "more People will die by Sea and Land [next year] than in all the World beside." Predictions of the same tenor and style are found in Rabelais's satirical almanac for 1533: *Pantagrueline prognostication certaine veritable et infalible,* printed at Lyons,[6] and in the parodistic English almanacs of the seventeenth and eighteenth centuries like *Poor Robin.* In the same class belong the remarks on the seasons or "Quarters" of the year which dwelt on such matters as the "great consumption in the purses of poets and almanack-makers" in the spring; the "Disease" known as "general laziness" prevalent in the summer; the unwelcome character of the autumn "to such persons as are to be hang'd"; and the diseases incident to winter, "want of money among the poor, and want of charity among some of the rich."[7] The readers seemed to have been fond of the "eclipse" and "seasons" type of humor, for it appeared often and in different almanacs.

The sections of the almanac giving various practical suggestions to the farmer and the housewife not infrequently included ridiculous recipes presented with mock seriousness. The thrifty reader, for instance, was told how "to keep warm a whole winter with one billet of wood." He was to go up to the garret with the piece of wood and throw it out of the window into the yard, then run downstairs as fast as he could, pick it up, and run up again at the same speed. This sequence of events was to be repeated until he had warmed up sufficiently, and the prescription was to be followed whenever he felt cold.[8] The neat housewife read that the best way to get rid of bugs was to catch them and cut their throats.[9]

Jokes constituted an important item in the humorous contents of the New York almanacs partly because they could be conveniently fitted into odds and ends of space. In some of the post-Revolutionary almanacs, they were set up vertically to fill up long narrow blank spaces left on the page by other printed matter, and, at first glance, look like columns of Chinese words. It was interesting to find certain popular types among them. The perennial pun is, of course, a conspicuous member, and usually occupies a safe Shakespearian level. One of the unfailing sources, indeed, was the cobbler's trade, with the inescapable "end," "awl," "last," and "sole" doing double duty on every possible occasion. An example from the *Hutchins* almanac for 1770 will suffice:

I would wish all maids to take a Husband whose name is

William, for when he is at home, she has her Will, and when he is abroad, she may take her Will.

Another popular type of humor was the familiar dream-device. This generally involved the winning of some kind of prize for telling the best story about an extraordinary dream. For example, two tradesmen and a clown who were traveling together shared their food supplies. At length, only a little flour was left, enough to make one cake. After wrangling for a day over who should get the cake, they decided to settle the dispute by agreeing that the man who could tell the strangest story would receive title to the property. The first tradesman then began by describing a dream in which he had visited Hell; the other tradesman recounted a dream in which he had taken a sightseeing tour through Heaven; and the clown concluded by telling them that he had dreamt they were both being carried off, so he had gotten up and eaten the cake.[10]

Tradesmen were not the only class who seemed to be a common subject for ridicule in the New York almanacs. The legal profession, the devotees of male fashions, the clergy, and the female sex were very popular targets. Numerous references to the clergy, however, did not make their appearance until the middle of the century.[11] In the main, they indicated popular doubt regarding the sincerity and usefulness of the clerical class. *Hutchins* would be glad if he found them "clear" of the eclipse of honesty predicted for the year 1756. Sailors and passengers were advised to lighten a ship during a storm by confessing their sins to the priest and then throwing him overboard.[12] *Poor Will*, for 1786 told the story of the preacher who had to interrupt a game of cards to deliver a sermon. Knowing the weakness of man, he took the two "hands" with him, concealing them in his sleeves. He was carried away during the sermon, and while he was in the midst of an energetic exhortation to his flock, the cards fell out. Without the least hesitation, he turned to one of the children in the congregation and asked him to step forward. He began to question him on the catechism. Under the circumstances, the child did poorly. Then the preacher asked him to identify the cards, and, with relief, the youngster did. Thereupon, the preacher concluded his sermon with a rousing peroration on the improper education of the young, who knew their cards better than their catechism.

Lawyers, judges, and the law were treated with scant respect. *Frank Freeman* for 1771 had a lyrical passage on the joy of the angels when they saw a lawyer entering heaven. And this picturesque "Description of a Country Sessions" appears in the *Hutchins* almanac for 1762:

Three or four parsons full of October,
Three or four 'squires between drunk and sober;

Three or four lawyers, three or four lyars;
Three or four constables, three or four cryers.
Three or four parishes bringing appeals,
Three or four writings, and three or four seals;
Three or four bastards, and three or four whores,
The rag and bob tail by three or four scores.
Three or four rum bulls and three or four cows,
Three or four orders and three or four bows,
Three or four old statutes not understood, . . .
Three or four roads that never were mended,
Three or four scolds, and the sessions is ended.

The New York almanacs often poked fun at extremes in fashion, both female and male, against which the prejudice of the people was reinforced in this country by religious and economic considerations. The towering headdress and hooped petticoat of the ladies and the adornments of the dainty fop were standard topics which, when the war with France came, were easily refurbished to serve as examples of the corruption and degeneration of the enemy. It was the vogue later in the century to present imaginary meetings of "boards of beaux" at which, for instance, they would vote to limit the amount of ribbon allowed on one foot to three yards and to confine the swagger within a space of three feet, nine inches.[13]

A large portion of the humor of the New York almanacs drew its sustenance from the subject of sex. In the main, about half of the jokes and humorous anecdotes and rhymes were inspired by this old preoccupation of man. In some issues, the joke section was exclusively sexual. As I have mentioned above, however, this humor was not pornographic but rather the naturalistic humor of the countryman. It generally reflected the patronizing and possessive attitude of the Colonial male toward the opposite sex, but there are signs to indicate that intransigent feminism was not altogether unknown in the colonies, as we may see by the joke about the independent young woman who refused during the marriage ceremony to promise to "obey" her future husband.[14] Other contemporary sources, too, showed considerable concern over the emergence, at about the mid-century, of the "masculine woman."[15]

The themes of the preservation of virginity and the universality of cuckoldry were the staple articles in this department of almanac humor. The importance of the guarantee of virginity was constantly being stressed. The stock situation was that of the man who was caught in the trap of his own devising. Having seduced many girls by promising to marry them, he finally succumbed to the first girl who was not taken in by the promise, only to discover after marriage that she had avoided making the mistake because of the lesson of experience. The proverbial complaisance of chambermaids was another standard source of jest and is illustrated by the anecdote of the stingy butcher. This butcher had paid his chambermaid a "Half-Joe" (Portuguese gold coin) for her kindness but demanded change the next morning. To avoid embarrassment, she gave him back the coin. A year later, when he happened to stop at the same tavern, he was arrested and charged with having put the township to the expense of bringing into the world and raising the maid's child. The judge ruled that he should pay the full amount of the expense plus a fine of forty pounds. As he was leaving the courtroom, the maid made this parting remark, "I hope, Sir, you have now got the Change for your Half-Joe."[16]

The faithlessness of wives was a theme of which the authors and readers of the New York almanacs never seemed to tire. The popular view is represented by the following selection from the *Hutchins* almanac for 1753:

> On a Market Day, comes an Archer by the Crowd, and necking an Arrow, as if he intended to shoot, said with a loud Voice, Now, have at a Cuckold; a Woman (thinking he levelled that Way, and her Husband being by her) cries out, Stand away Husband, stand away Husband; why, you silly Jade, quoth he, I am no Cuckold, am I? No, no, quoth she; but you don't know how a playing Arrow may glance.

In general, it was dangerous to rely on the constancy of women and very foolish to allow oneself to be placed under the yoke of love, for then one lost all independence and life was unendurable. The almanacs frequently published humorous "cures" for love to help their male readers, of which the following from the *Hutchins* almanac for 1762 is a sample:

> Take eight ounces of Consideration, half the quantity of Indifference, ten grains of Ingratitude, six scruples of Patience, a small sprig of Rue, two good handfulls of Employment, four months Absence, mixt with the frequent conversation of a pretty Rival; to this you must add as much Discretion as nature has allotted you. Boil them all together, till a third part be consumed, cooling them with a few slights, spread them upon the thoughts of your Mistress's imperfections, and apply the plaister to your heart (but be sure not to take it off till it falls off of itself) . . . .

A female type very dear to almanac humor was the married shrew, about whom there was unceasing lamentation. In many

humorous pieces she also was made to typify the unfaithful wife, as
in this rhyme:

> I'll list for a soldier, says Robin to Sue,
> To avoid your eternal Disputes;
> Aye, aye, cried the Termagant, do, Robin, do;
> I'll raise the mean while, fresh Recruits.[17]

One of the best specimens of this type is "A Comical Adventure between a Cobler, his Wife, and a Chimney-Sweeper," in the *Hutchins*
almanac for 1762. The tale, written with Rabelaisian gusto, deals with
the nocturnal experiences of a befuddled Crispin whose noisy spouse
had chased him out of the house late one night as he returned from a
drinking bout. A chimney sweep who had overheard her send her
husband to the devil pretended to be that personage and had a good
deal of fun at the husband's expense and much pleasure on his own
account before finally patching up a truce between the couple. The
best part of the story describes the husband's coming back home after
being assured by the "devil" that his mate had been whisked off to
hell. In reality she was concealed in a closet. He entered his bedroom
singing gaily and, as he undressed, hummed an old ballad to himself:

> I value not silver or gold,
> Now I'm rid of a troublesome evil;
> My wife was a damnable scold,
> But now she is gone to the devil.

At that moment she rushed from the closet, crying:

> "You lie, you rogue, I defy the devil and all his works, I
> will make you know, sirrah, there is never a devil in hell
> can master me, if I am set on't; you may see by my
> pickle, I was forced to struggle hard to overcome Satan;
> and since I have conquered the devil I am resolved I'll
> master you!"

The poor shoemaker was reduced to hopelessness and "forced to cry
peccavi."

It is too bad that we have no almanacs of that period written
from the woman's point of view. If we did, we might have amusing
portraits of bullies to match those of shrews, and of male virginity
and fidelity from the woman's angle. In the absence of these we must
be content with such rare anecdotes as the following, which give at
least a hint of the feminine point of view.

An esteemed farmer lost his cow and his wife within a

short time. His neighbors, to comfort him, offered him daughters, sisters, and nieces to take the place of his dead wife. "Lord have mercy on us [replied the farmer] it is better to lose one's wife than one's cow; my wife is hardly three hours dead, and here are half a dozen people already offering to supply her place for me; but when my cow died, the devil a one spoke of giving me another."[18]

Since most of the readers of the Colonial almanacs were farmers with limited education and very little money, a good part of almanac humor was calculated to appeal to them. It fostered a populist rural bias in American humor that was predominant until the present century; and it was cultivated by men like Daniel Leeds and his successors, Nathaniel Ames and Poor Richard, who were the first of the native breed of distinctively American commentators on the contemporary scene that have long reflected the lack of reverence of the common people of this country for fellow men above them and often for themselves.

Part Two

EDUCATION OF THE COMMON PEOPLE

CHAPTER 6

The Way of Righteousness

With this chapter we turn to an examination of those features of the New York almanacs that indicate how they attempted to mold the opinion and widen the outlook of their readers. The Bible, which had been practically the only source of mental nourishment for most of the colonists during the seventeenth century, was supplemented in the next century by a book that looked to the present instead of the past and sought to bring its readers something of the activity and thought of the contemporary world. It is remarkable how many of the important tendencies of the period were represented in the almanac selections, and it is reasonable to suppose that the impression made by these selections was intensified by the state of insulation in which most of the colonists found themselves. The average Colonial household being in a sense marooned, the arrival of the annual almanac was an event as exciting as the visit of a traveler from the civilized world, and it was undoubteldy examined with as much curiosity and eagerness as such a visitor would have encountered. Moreover, the, popular reverence for the printed word gave it an authority which no ordinary traveler could hope to possess.

Religion

One of the best illustrations of the use of the almanac as "a vehicle for conveying instruction among the common people" is the religious controversy that raged for more than a decade in the almanacs of Daniel Leeds. The spark that set it ablaze was thrown by George Keith in Philadelphia soon after 1690, but the combustible material had been accumulating for many years, from the time when the Quakers had first formulated a complete system of organization and discipline. Ever since then, there had been a division of opinion between those who followed the word and those who trusted in the "inward Christ." In Pennsylvania the division was widened by the fact that some of the Quakers were also the civil authorities and had to deal with situations where principle and reality were hard to reconcile. It appears that the ruling faction leaned toward the doctrine of the "inward Christ," perhaps because it was more flexible, while Keith wished to establish a written creed. His disappointment at not having been recognized as leader on the death of George Fox in 1690 may have sharpened the edge of his opposition,[1] as the fear of losing power may have encouraged his enemies to take extreme measures against him and his adherents.[2] As a matter of fact, there were so many Quakers who sympathized with his views that his enemies in Philadelphia might not have been able to oust him from their community if he had been less contentious and more tactful.[3] When he was "in a transport of heat and passion," he too frequently called some of "his brethren in the ministry, and other elders, and that upon small provocation (if any), fools, ignorant heathens, infidels, silly souls, liars, heretics, rotten ranters, Muggletonians, and other names of that infamous strain".[4] On the other hand, the conduct of the Quaker authorities of Philadelphia during the heat of the conflict was not above criticism and compels one to doubt the accuracy of Parrington's idyllic picture of the early Quaker colony

> . . . where Quaker and Lutheran dwelt together in peace if not in fellowship [since] they were New Testament men and not of the Old, like the Saints in Massachusetts Bay. They worshipped a God of love rather than a God of wrath.[5]

In the almanac for 1695, *Daniel Leeds* charged the Quakers with "taking away Goods, and imprisoning some, and condemning others without Tryal, for Religious discent." He was referring to the incident which climaxed the battle between Keith and the authorities. In 1692 Keith had finally been denounced in the Philadelphia Meeting for his hostile writings and his abusive treatment of other Quakers, and had thereupon appealed his case to the General Meeting. However, he wrote and had Bradford print a summary of his grievances, which was distributed before the General Meeting. This was viewed both as unethical and dangerous, and the authorities arrested Bradford and several others of Keith's party, the former for printing a seditious pamphlet, the rest for distributing it. Four quarto pages of type and some books that were in Bradford's printing shop were seized. According to Daniel Leeds's *News of a Trumpet*, John Macombe, after his arrest, was not permitted to go home to take leave of his family although "his wife was but two days delivered of a child and in danger of death by a flux, and another of his family sick also that dyed a short time after."[6]

The story of the judicial proceedings was told by Bradford in a pamphlet ironically entitled *New England Spirit of Persecution* and printed in New York in 1693. The court consisted of six Quaker justices and two non-Quaker magistrates. When the Quaker justices refused to allow Keith and the others to defend themselves at the hearing, the non-Quaker magistrates withdrew. The court, declaring that it "could judge of matter of fact without evidence," then found Keith "to be a seditious person, and an enemy to the king and queen's government." The denunciation also mentioned his criticism of the authorities for proceeding against certain privateers with "the carnal sword," a criticism doubly painful because it was true.

At his trial several months later, Bradford defended himself by advancing a liberal interpretation of the law of libel which departed radically from the legal opinion of the time. The government maintained that the function of the jury was restricted to determining whether or not Bradford had printed the seditious pamphlet. Bradford argued that the jury must also decide whether the pamphlet was seditious. The obviously biased judges were much annoyed by Bradford's skillful defense. He was reminded that it was the winter season and that the judges would endanger their health if he continued to prolong the trial by his tricks. When the jury could not agree, an officer was commanded to keep them confined in the jury room without fire, food, drink, and tobacco until they could think more clearly. This jury, however, was beyond redemption and was finally discharged, but Bradford, who had been in prison since his arrest, was not released. Several months later he was suddenly set free, perhaps because the frame of type, the chief piece of evidence against him, was accidentally destroyed, but more probably because Governor Fletcher had interceded in his behalf. Soon after, his equipment was restored to him, and he moved his printing shop to New York. The Bradford trial deserves to occupy a conspicuous place in the early history of the struggle for the freedom of the American press, particularly in its relation to the celebrated trial of John Peter Zenger, who was one of Bradford's apprentices and probably was impressed at an early age by the story of his master's trial.[7]

Bradford and Daniel Leeds, after the former's removal from Philadelphia, followed the example of Keith after his banishment from the Society of Friends and transferred their allegiance to the Church of England. To what extent Bradford's decision was affected by Fletcher's devotion to the Episcopal cause, it is impossible to say. However that may be, the fact is that the *Daniel Leeds* almanacs of New York, almost from the beginning, took an active part in the attempt of the Church of England to win over the disaffected followers of Keith among the Quakers, many of whom lived on Long Island and in Westchester County. In the 1695 issue Daniel Leeds declared that his attacks on the Quakers were directed only against the "heathen and Persecuting" ones, and predicted "a blessing on

Philadelphia" in the immediate future, which, as he explained two years later, assumed the shape of a minister of the Church of England. Soon after George Keith returned to this country as a missionary for the Church of England, the *Daniel Leeds* almanacs turned from general criticism of the intolerance of the anti-Keithian Quakers to specific criticism of the principles of the Quaker religion and advocacy and elucidation of the Episcopal creed. That Leeds and Bradford were directly cooperating in the campaign of Keith is indicated by a statement in the *Daniel Leeds* almanac for 1706, taunting the Quakers for refusing to accept Keith's challenges to public debate.

The *Daniel Leeds* almanac for 1704 attacked the Quaker doctrine on the questions of circumcision, baptism, and the ministry. Furthermore, a flank attack was made on the claim that Quakers preached "freely"; in support, the revelations of a former member of the Society[8] were used to cite several examples of preachers who had risen from poverty to wealth: George Fox, who "from a Journey-man Shoe-maker, turned Quaker-Preacher, travell'd the world, and dyed worth more than the late Arch-Bishop of Canterbury"; Stephen Crisp, who had been a poor Weaver; W. Bingly, a poor tailor; "Tho. Green," who "from a poor Brick-layer dyed worth Thousands"; and Samuel Waldenfield, "formerly a Glasier now a vast Rich Draper in London." These instances of worldly success attending conversion to the Quaker religion were dangerous weapons to handle, for it is not improbable that they made as many Quakers as they unmade.

The statement in the *Philadelphia Almanack* for 1705 by Caleb Pusey, a prominent writer and mill owner of Pennsylvania, to the effect that the Quakers had not departed from their early principles, offered a challenge that was quickly taken up by Leeds in his next almanac. He refuted Pusey's assertion on four counts:

1. The Quakers, in order to win converts, no longer emphasized their opposition to baptism.
2. They no longer enforced the rule that no Quaker should hold office or place of trust or profit in the government.
3. They no longer accepted the Scriptures as of "Divine Authority."
4. They no longer fought merely with "spiritual Weapons."

All these changes indicated a conservative tendency that should have made conversion to the Episcopal creed not very difficult; some of the examples were presented most forcefully. Referring to the 1695 grant to William Penn for Pennsylvania, which stipulated that he must either send eighty soldiers to New York on demand or pay for the maintenance of that number, Leeds asked whether the Quakers would send "spiritual Souldiers" or "spiritual Money." He also told about the Quaker Mead who, upon being attacked by three highwaymen, knocked them down and beat them with an oak staff. Mead later defended his conduct and explained his strength as follows: "Verily, Friends, the Spirit of the Lord came upon me, and I could have fought with seven Men."

The copy of the *Daniel Leeds* almanac for 1706 in the John Carter Brown Library contains a long supplementary article on Quaker preaching that is not found in the copy belonging to the New York Historical Society. The article called the Quaker method of preaching "bewitchment," and the author recalled that he once attended a Meeting where the Dutch Quaker Telner stirred his listeners to a high pitch of religious fervor, although not one of them understood the Dutch language in which he spoke. Moreover, the use of women preachers was decried on the ground that Christ had not appointed any female apostles and that the danger of "bewitchment" was so much greater. The author did not fail to include a few of the usual anecdotes about the loose moral life led by some of the Quaker preachers, but did not confine the stories to either sex.

So much for the negative and destructive work. The almanac for 1705, on the other hand, was devoted to setting forth the doctrine of the Church of England in persuasive form. Moreover, a conciliatory invitation was extended to the Presbyterians, Independents, and "better sort of Baptists" to attend the exposition. This concerned itself with establishing the necessity of "an outward Commission to Gospel Ministers," the value of prayer, the harm caused by irresponsible preaching, and "the legitimate scriptural sources of the Common Prayer." Presumably, Daniel Leeds gave prominence to the matter of prayer because of the sensible Quaker objection to fixed times of prayer. For the benefit of those converted, the almanac also contained "Observations on the Holy and Festival Days."

It appears, though, that the strivings of Keith and his followers did not meet with much success, partly perhaps because the Episcopal party had the misfortune in some cases to be led by such scoundrels as Lord Cornbury. Keith himself admits failure, but adds: "However, I am not without hope that the Seed that God had enabled me to Sow among them, will in some of them, in due time, take Root downward, and bear Fruit upward, though little of it doth yet appear."[9]

The memory of the Keith conflict undoubtedly played a large part in making Daniel Leeds an advocate of religious toleration. He frequently denounced the unchristian persecution of Christians for nonconformity and often expressed the hope that the time would come when all differences would be ironed out and all Christians would be members of one Church—although he trusted that this church would be not unlike the Church of England. The example set by him was followed and improved upon during the century. His son, Titan, introduced a new note of sympathy and understanding toward heresy well summed up in the maxim: "True Zeal extends more Charity to a Heretick than to a Sinner."[10] A rationalistic point of view developed in the New York almanacs at the midcentury, which the following rhyme illustrates:

> The priestly office cannot be deny'd
> It wears heaven's livery, and is made our guide;
> But why should we be punished if we stray,
> When our guides dispute which is the way.[11]

This spirit of tolerance was evident in the almanacs of other colonies. We read, for example, in a Massachusetts almanac:

> All Faiths are to their own Believers just,
> For none believe because they will but must;
> By Education most have been misled,
> So they believe because they were so bred.[12]

It must be observed, however, that the New York almanacs did not practice what they preached in the case of the Roman Catholic Church, the mistrust and hatred of which had been apparently too deeply impressed to be eradicated in the short space of a century. There was not even a hint of softening toward Rome, not a single friendly word for it in all the New York almanacs or any of the other almanacs I read. On the contrary, what was written could only tend to keep alive the spirit of animosity and even to intensify it. The bitter struggle between England and France for world dominance in this century surely fanned the flame. In England, the almanacs were no less hostile during these years.[13]

In the New York almanacs the antagonism to the "papists" expressed itself in three ways: recollection, insult, or prophecy, according as the attention was fixed on the past, the present, or the future, respectively. An illustration of the second type is a letter from the "Hon. William Hamilton" describing the great eruption of Mount Vesuvius on October 10, 1767, and the ridiculous and vulgar manifestations of religious superstition among the people of Naples during the catastrophe, particularly in their treatment of their patron saint, Januarius, who was loaded with coarse abuse during the eruption and cheap gratitude after it.[14] The third type was very common and took the form of predicting that the end of the papacy and "popery" was imminent. The preface to *Titan Leeds* for 1738 contains a typical specimen, connected with the author's remarks on notable conjunctions of Saturn and Jupiter which were scheduled to occur in 1742 and 1763:

> Perhaps then will be the beginning of pouring forth of

the seven Vials or last Plagues upon Babylon or Tyrus, i.e. the Papacy . . . about the Time above-mentioned we may expect that the Prophecy of Isaiah . . . will be fulfilled upon her, viz. "And strangers shall stand and feed your Flocks, and Aliens shall be your plowmen and your Vine-dressers, and ye shall eat the Riches of the Gentiles . . . ."

Probably the most effective type was the first, since it included tales of atrocities inflicted on Protestants by the Inquisition. Aspersions on the Jesuit order belong in this category. Consider, for example, these verses from the *Felix Leeds* almanac for 1730:

> No Jesuit e'er took in Hand
> To plant a Church in barren Land
> And where there is no Store of Wealth
> Souls are not worth the Charge of Health;
> Spain, in America, had two Designs,
> To sell their Gospel, get their Mines;
> For had the Mexicans been poor
> No Jesuit twice had landed on their Shore.

Toward the close of the war with France *Roger More,* 1762 printed an article on the Inquisition, entitled "The Pope's Practice of Piety," the purpose of which, expressly stated at the end, was to warn the English that they must expect similar treatment if they were defeated and had to admit popery into England. The practice of the Inquisitors, according to this count, was to place the suspected heretic on the rack, after he had denied his guilt at three examinations. The devices of torture were described in detail. If he still persisted in his denial, and very few did after the first experience of the rack, he was taken back to his cell, where a surgeon was at hand "to put his Bones in joint." He was later subjected to the rack a second time, and, if he still maintained his innocence, a third time. If he sought escape from agony by admitting what his tormentors wanted him to admit, he was brought back to the rack, so that they might discover who his teachers and accomplices were. During all this he was kept in ignorance of the charge against him and of the name of his accuser and was not allowed to have his own counsel. It was naturally useless to call witnesses to certify his innocence because defense of a suspected heretic might lead the witness himself to the rack. Suicide was considered evidence of guilt. A significant corollary of the condemnation of a heretic was the provision that his estate was thereby forfeited to the Inquisition. Moreover, the Inquisition could try a man for heresy after his death unless he had been dead more than forty years. The article concluded with a gruesome depiction of the burning of heretics, which always took place on Sunday morning. The procession of the doomed wearing black coats upon which flames and monsters were painted, the unholy glee of the populace, who preferred these spectacles to "a Bull-Feast, or a Farce," and the differences in length of torment of the condemned caused by the condition of the wind were graphically portrayed. The punishment was, of course, carried out by the secular arm, which the church always urged to be lenient, although it was understood that failure to impose the death sentence by burning would expose the offending authorities to arrest by the Inquisition as "Favourers of Hereticks." But the author conceded that the inhuman joy of the spectators was "not an Effect of the natural Cruelty of these Peoples' Dispositions, but the Spirit of their Religion against Protestants." It is easy to imagine the incendiary effect of articles like these on the imagination of the common people of this country.

While the New York almanacs did not, strictly speaking, take a definite stand, as in the case of Catholics or Quakers, they made a considerable contribution to the Great Awakening, the wave of religious enthusiasm which rose and fell in the colonies during the half-century before the Revolution. Their pages abounded in apocalyptic visions of the end of the world, reports of angels coming down to earth to warn sinners of the wrath of God, stories of extraordinary journeys to the realms of bliss, and announcements of miracles of the Lord's goodness. It is true that some of these events took place in faraway places like Italy and Russia, but a few were witnessed as near home as Philadelphia, and at Medford in Massachusetts. Mr. Thomas Say of Philadelphia was in a trance for eight hours, during which he left his body and rose to heaven where he was "cloathed in white, and in my full Shape, without the least Diminution of Parts." There he met a black named Coffee, belonging to the Widow Kearney, who also was garbed "in a Garment of unsullied white." When he awoke in Philadelphia, he immediately mentioned the time and circumstances of Coffee's death, to the amazement of his audience, for Coffee had really died.[15] Ebenezer Adams of Medford was the man deemed worthy of a visit from three angels on the night of February 4, 1761. They entered at the door of his bedchamber, wearing "Crowns on their Heads which glissen'd like Stars." Then one of them delivered a beautiful sermon for an hour on the fourth verse of the third chapter of Paul's Epistle to the Colossians, part of which Ebenezer wrote down later from memory. The theme of the sermon was, in the words of the angel, "Remember the great Judge is now frowning in an awful Manner on this sinful and wicked world."[16] Adams, in conclusion, exhorted his readers in this manner: "Oh! the great God has been inviting us a long Time to forsake our Sins, and turn unto Him by Repentance, thro' the Merits and Meditation of Jesus our Redeemer."

At the same time, the influence of rationalism continued to challenge the authority of the Scriptures. An item in the *Thomas More* almanac for 1766 indicates that the authority of the Scriptures, no longer unchallenged among the people, sought support in the new science. In this article the miracle of the sun's standing still for the benefit of Joshua was referred to the fact that an eclipse recorded by the Chinese in the year 2155 BC was twelve hours out of line with modern calculations. The discrepancy could be easily explained by accepting the truth of the Biblical miracle. The resort to science was a dangerous step, encouraging the process of submitting not only the less credible elements of the Scriptures but also Christianity itself to the test of rational analysis. One result of this examination is reflected in an essay entitled "False notions of Providence," printed in the *Father Hutchins* almanac for 1792, which set forth the deistic principle that Providence does not interpose directly in human affairs or change the course of nature because of an individual or the human race. In the opinion of the author of the essay, the belief in such direct action or interest on the part of Deity "argues pride and arrogance in man; and disparages the moral character of the great Parent of the Universe."

Throughout our period the almanacs found it necessary to make frequent sallies against atheism, a fact that suggests that it was not uncommon. The method of attack consisted either in categorical affirmations of the folly of its professors or illustrations of their insincerity. In the earlier period the former were more often employed; witness *Daniel Leeds* asserting in verse that the men who said there was no God were fools, those who proclaimed this belief publicly were even greater fools, but the greatest fools of all were the ones whose actions betrayed this belief. His honesty, however, made him add: "such Fools are we."[17] The second method of attack is illustrated by the story in the *Hutchins* almanac for 1780 about a "Free-thinker" who confessed his error during a storm at sea but recanted when he reached land safely. Some time later he was wounded in a duel and again confessed his heresy. Unfortunately he recovered and relapsed for the second time.

In general religious topics occupied less and less space in the New York almanacs as the years passed, and after the time of Daniel Leeds were relegated to the background by the material on science and politics and the other interests of the period. This tendency continued even during the period of the Great Awakening. The religious pulse remained normal and regular, except during the early fever of the Quaker squabble and the excitement of the war with Catholic France. Poems were printed now and then in praise of God, but these came alive only when they referred to His incomprehensible greatness as a cosmic Architect. The occasional exhortations to piety and virtue were perfunctory. The minister had become a member of one of the professions deriving his authority from his mind and character rather than his station. He was scrutinized critically and, if found wanting, was unhesitatingly reviled. The conservative *Hutchins* almanac could print with impunity in 1755:

> What makes all Doctrines plain and clear?
> About Two Hundred Pound a Year.
> And that which was prov'd true before,
> Prov'd false again?—Two Hundred more.

In another issue we read:

> How unnatural a sight it is to see a parson with a florid countenance and double chin, preach up abstinence in time of Lent.[18]

By the time of the Revolution the tide of popular indifference or active hostility to organized religion had probably risen so high that some of the almanac-authors became alarmed. The almanac issued by the Revolutionary printer Samuel Loudon for 1781 deplored the lack of religion in that "libertine age" and ascribed many of the contemporary social and economic ills to this phenomenon. He earnestly appealed to Americans to give up Sabbath-breaking and free thinking and seek peace and prosperity in the Lord.

Education

At the beginning of the eighteenth century the town and province of New York were, to say the least, indifferent to the education of their citizens. The Reverend John Sharpe of New York wrote in 1713 that there was no "city" in America where learning was less encouraged. Children were taught little more than writing and arithmetic, and the teaching of "letters" was regarded as superfluous. The reason for this state of affairs was, in his estimation, the fact that the "City is so conveniently situated for Trade and the Genius of the people so inclined to merchandise."[19] Almost twenty years before, Daniel Leeds had noted the same thing and had remarked in the preface to his almanac for 1695:

> I should be glad to see Learning and Knowledge more improved than it is either in Divinity, Law, Physick, Mathematicks, or Grammar; but instead of these laudable Sciences, in too many places the *Punch Bowle* and *Tobacco-Box* is accounted a better Companion than a Library of good Books.

It is not improbable that when he wrote this preface he had already conceived the idea of improving the learning and knowledge of those who read the almanac by making it a sort of compact "library of good books." The idea was a good one, and practical. The readers did not have to pay for the extra features, and he could sell more almanacs if he gave something away for nothing with them. In this way, also, the cause of education would be served.

Formal education continued, however, to reflect the preoccupation of the people with the business of making a living, and, if possible, of accumulating wealth. The almanacs confirm this. For example, William Ball of Bordertown, New Jersey, advertising his private school in an almanac for 1735, announced that he taught "Reading, Writing, Arithmetic, vulgar and decimal Mensuration, Geometry, Trigonometry, Gaging, Surveying, Navigation, Astronomy, Dialling, and Book-keeping, both single and according to the Italian Method, or double Entry." Nevertheless, he thought it necessary to include this statement: "No Money demanded untill the Learner be instructed."[20] John Nathan Hutchins conducted a similar school "at the Corner of Beaver-Street, in New York" in 1753, and advertised it in his almanac for that year and several times during the following years. *Thomas More*, 1750, even under these conditions, thought that many a boy who showed no desire for "Learning or Study" was compelled to pursue his education beyond the elementary stage, "and by that means Time and Money is spent upon him in vain, as there's too many such Boobies in the World." The *Wing* almanac for 1762 advocated a more practical education for women who had little or no money to bring their husbands. The most frequently advertised book in the New York almanacs of the century was *The Young Man's Companion*, which included directions for spelling, reading, and writing "True English," made arithmetic easy, taught the method of writing good business and personal letters, and printed "a choice Collection" of legal forms.

On the other hand, the New York almanacs sometimes imitated the example of *Daniel Leeds* and urged upon their readers the benefits to be gained from a general education. They were told that a man never opened a book without reaping some advantage from it.[21] Circulating libraries were advertised not only in the pocket almanacs and almanac-registers but also in the general almanacs. For instance, Samuel Loudon's circulating library of about two thousand volumes was advertised in the *New York and Country Almanack* for 1776, which stated that it was open daily from morning until evening, both to members, who paid an annual fee of five dollars, and nonmembers, who paid a loan fee for each book equal to about 8 percent of the book's value. Persons living in New York City could draw one book at a time; those living out of town, two or three. These terms were very liberal for the time and made the library available to a wider circle of readers than was then generally the case. The more successful New York Society Library fifteen years later was less generous, charging an annual membership fee of more than twenty-five dollars and keeping open daily only from noon until two o'clock. It is true, however, that the great majority of almanac readers, even if they had wished, were prevented for economic or geographic reasons from availing themselves of these facilities.

A few years after the middle of the century, the New York almanacs began to manifest a new interest in children and their education. Proverbs, stories, and essays were devoted to reminding parents how important the period of childhood was and telling them what to do and what to avoid during this period, since

> Children like tender Oziers take the Bow
> And as they first are fashion'd always grow.[22]

For the first time we observe the beginning of a sympathetic attitude and a psychological approach in facing the problem of their education. For instance, an essay in the *Thomas More* almanac for 1767, which discussed the theme of discipline, advised parents to exercise prudent leniency if they wished to gain the cooperation of their children and asked them to remember their own childhood and be guided by their recollections of the mistakes and injustices committed by their elders against them. To see this essay in proper perspective, one must set it against specimens of the "advice" given to children in the earlier primers, of which the following is a sample:

> Children, consider that you may Dye, as Young as you are; you may see Graves in the Field shorter than the smallest of you all. Consider, that you may Perish, as young as you are there are small Chips as well as great Logs in the Fire of Hell . . . Let this Thought encourage you: There are more Children in Heaven than of any other Age.[23]

Incidentally, the use of fear as a means of discipline and education was deprecated in the almanacs.

The *Roger More* almanac for 1761, in a long essay entitled "Of Education," brought together most of the views on this subject scattered through the almanacs of the time. The essay was concerned only with the education of children. The author, after establishing the thesis that the end of education was the health of the body and the improvement of the mind, divided his essay accordingly into two parts. The first part contained sensible instructions on the physical care of the child; the second part stressed the permanence of impressions made during infancy and childhood, pointing out the wisdom of "seasoning their Minds as soon as possible with the Tincture of Virtue and Religion," and ending with a story illustrating the baneful effect of frightening children. Particular attention was paid in the almanacs to the topic of the proper care of infants. The frequent nursing of babies, particularly during the night, and the habit of rocking them to sleep came in for much adverse comment.[24] The point of view and state of knowledge of the period was aptly expressed in an article which appeared in the *Thomas More* almanac for 1768. The author, holding that the practice of rocking infants to sleep was bad for their health, argued that nature seemed to have intended them to rest generally "in a kind of lethargic composure, which contributes to ripen and perfect the organs," and that parents should not prevent them, when they began to cry, from "paying their tribute to nature":

> Would it not be better to leave them to themselves, and let them sink gradually into the calm condition to which the fatigue of spirits would presently reduce them?

Passages like these show that the New York almanac was part of the great movement in the reformation of education whose crest Rousseau was then riding.

The importance attached to the education of the young must have conferred a new dignity upon the profession of teaching. If, as one almanac declared, "all the Happiness and Glory of a State depends on the Education of Youth,"[25] it followed that the teaching profession was one of the most important in New York, and teachers must be selected with great care. An essay in *Father Hutchins's* almanac for 1776, which dealt with the "Qualifications . . . for a Teacher of Children," found that they were: good family, fine personality, great patience, neat appearance, sound learning, and experience. The idea that any misfit or incompetent who had a little book knowledge could supervise the education of children, or that education was simply a matter of memorizing facts evidently was on the wane. The people had not yet reached the point where they were ready and willing to pay for better education, and teachers still had to perform an amusing variety of extra services to eke out a bare living,[26] but the basic social value of education was beginning to be recognized, and that was a great step forward.

The almanacs had little to say on the subject of higher education, but the New York almanac-registers have preserved a good deal of interesting contemporary information about early American colleges, particularly the college which has grown into Columbia University. In *Gaine's Universal Register* for 1775 it was called "New-York College" and was thus described:

> The Building (which is only one Third of the intended Structure) consists of an elegant Stone Edifice, three complete Stories high, with four Stair-cases, twelve

apartments in each, a Chapel, Hall, Library, Museum, Anatomical Theatre and a School for experimental Philosophy. All Students, but those in Medicine, are obliged to lodge and diet in the College . . . . The Edifice is surrounded by an high Fence, which also encloses a large Court and Garden; and a Porter constantly attends at the front Gate, which is lock'd at 10 o'clock each Evening in Summer, and at 9 in Winter; after which Hours, the Names of all that come in, are delivered weekly to the President. The College is situated on dry gravelly Soil about 150 Yards from the Bank of Hudson's River, which it overlooks; commanding a most extensive and beautiful Prospect.

It was announced and emphasized that the college, which required no religious test of its fellows, tutors, and professors, offered the advantages of higher education to students of all denominations.

An idea of the expenses at the college in those days may be gained from *Gaine's* register for 1791, which stated that board cost about one dollar and fifty cents a week, and that the tuition fee was five dollars a year for each course. The requirements for admission given in the same register were no less remarkable. The student had to be

able to render into English, Caesar's Commentaries of the Gallic War; the four Orations of Cicero against Catiline; the first four books of Virgil's Aeneid; and the gospels from the Greek; and to explain the government and connection of the words, and to turn English into grammatical Latin, and must understand the first four rules of arithmetic, with the rule of three, and vulgar and decimal fractions.

Moral Reform

Throughout the century the New York almanacs raised their voices against the contemporary evil of excessive drinking, at first perfunctorily, but after the middle of the century, with increasing vigor and fervor. In the *Leeds* almanacs the objections were confined mainly to the idea that it was uneconomical. In the case of women, drunkenness was denounced as an additional enemy in the unceasing battle for the maintenance of virtue. By drunkenness, of course, was meant a state of intoxication similar to the one described in a popular rhyme of the century:

Figure 2. A South East View of the City of New York, c. 1763.

> Not drunk is he who from the floor
> Can rise again and still drink more,
> But drunk is he who prostrate lies
> Without the power to drink or rise.[27]

Beginning with the middle of the century, intemperance was attacked as a social evil undermining the health and wealth of the people. Essays and stories offered sad instances of the gradual decline and ruin of men who yielded to the vice.[28]

The New York almanacs did not always assume a serious attitude on the question. Sometimes the convivial spirit, which was more common in the English almanacs, got the upper hand, and the readers would be presented with such gay trifles as the following:

> Dr. Aldrick's five Reasons for Drinking:
> Good Wine; a Friend; or, being dry;
> Or, lest we should be by and by;
> Or, any other Reason why.[29]

The problem of black slavery was almost completely ignored by the New York almanacs of the Colonial period. In some of the lists of population figures, the blacks were listed separately. In the pocket almanac and almanac-registers after the Revolution, the "Society for promoting the Manumission of Slaves" was frequently mentioned, and *Gaine's* pocket almanac for 1787 announced the prohibition of the slave trade in New York by the law of April 12, 1785, but nothing that could be interpreted as an expression of opinion appeared until 1793. In that year, two New York almanacs, *Greenleaf's* and *Father Hutchins,* showed an unprecedented interest in the lot of the black slave—the former with a poem, "Humanity, or the Rights of Nature" by Pratt, and the latter with a selection from James Anderson's *Bee.* Both pieces are of the sentimental type of literature popular at the time.

There are sporadic protests in the New York almanacs against the use of tobacco and the practice of "gaming."[30] In 1700 *Daniel Leeds* had referred to rum and tobacco as "two enemies to the Publick," and the same opinion was echoed here and there among his successors. *Copernicus,* in his almanac for 1747, expressed the hope that the authorities would "make a vig'rous Stand" against gambling. Even Mahomet, good Christian readers were informed by *Hutchins,* 1778, forbade it in the Koran. But the crusading and reforming spirit of the nineteenth century had not yet touched the almanacs, except in the education of the young. Circumstances and the reaction against religious emotionalism had ushered in an age in which scientific inquiry and political and economic pioneering were predominant. Religion was no longer a striving to come nearer to God and ultimate reality, but a formal doctrine which one was taught in childhood and to which one paid lip service for the rest of his life. It really did not matter what doctrine one subscribed to, provided it included the recognition of a Supreme Deity and encouraged one to lead a useful and moral life. The emphasis had been shifted from man's relation to God and rested now on man's relation to nature and his fellow men. The mental energies released from theology by the Reformation, and for a time occupied with the problem of finding the real place of man in the universal scheme of things, were turned to the observation of nature and society, and men, with a great thrill, embarked on voyages of exploration and discovery into unknown seas and dark continents.

CHAPTER 7

Popular Science and Superstition

The function of the Colonial almanac of the eighteenth century as an instructor of the common people is clearly demonstrated by that part of its contents which nowadays would be labelled "popular science." This feature of the almanac was a natural extension of its original function as a calendar, one of the first and greatest of scientific inventions. In approaching the "scientific" side of the almanac during that century, one must remember that the domain of science at that time was not laid out and subdivided as neatly as it is today. The boundaries between science and philosophy, science and conjecture, and one science and another were not as well defined. Moreover, in justice to the past, we should keep in mind that the science of one generation is sometimes the superstition of the next. Then again, certain traditional items of pseudoscience, such as the man of signs and the weather predictions, continued to be published because of popular demand long after the almanac-authors themselves had indicated that they had no value.

In the New York almanacs the most important "sciences" of the century, physics, astronomy, medicine, botany, and astrology, were well represented. A good deal of the instruction in them was, of course, of a practical kind, intended for use: for the physician, remedies and medical articles; for the farmer, advice on agricultural matters; for his wife, suggestions for the care of health and remedies in case of illness. On the other hand, much of the information could serve no other purpose than to increase the reader's general knowledge and widen his mental horizon. *Roger Sherman's* almanac for 1754, for instance, contained an introductory lesson on the earth and its atmosphere, which included only one item of possible utility—an explanation of how a pump worked. For the rest, the reader learned that the earth consisted of earth, water, and air; that air was "a flued which is compressible and delateable, but can never be congealed and fixed," and that it was essential for life, combustion, and sound; that sound was produced by "vibration of the Air" and traveled at the speed of 1142 feet a second; that wind was due either to the expansion of air by heat or its contraction by cold; and that storms at the equator resulted from the heat of the sun. He would be an ingenious reader, indeed, who could find a practical application for this sort of instruction. In the main, New York almanacs passed on to their readers the principal scientific interests of the Colonial period, with the exception of electricity, which was the rage at midcentury.

During the twenty-five years preceding the Revolution, there arose and developed in the colonies an enthusiastic movement for the improvement of farming.[1] Standard texts on the subject, such as John Worledge's *The Mystery of Husbandry Discovered*, were imported in considerable numbers, and original Colonial studies, like Jared Eliot's essays on "field husbandry," the first of which appeared in 1748, were immensely successful. As a result, Colonial farmers were encouraged not only to try the suggestions of the authorities, but also to initiate their own experiments. In New York they were helped by the "Society for promoting Arts, Agriculture, and Oeconomy," which offered valuable cash prizes for exceptional achievements. Quite naturally, the almanacs undertook to keep the small farmers, who could not afford to buy books, in touch with the movement, and acted as a medium for the exchange of knowledge among their more enterprising farmer-readers. The New York almanacs from the very beginning had included suggestions on farming, and it was easy for them to expand this service. As one reads these old recommendations, he observes at first hand the difficulties and problems which had to be faced in converting the wilderness into life-supporting and wealth-producing farmland and appreciates how much the almanac assisted in the task.

I found the following matters most frequently taken up in the New York almanacs: The raising of cows,[2] horses,[3] and sheep,[4] the growing of wheat[5] and flax,[6] the cultivation of orchards,[7] and the methods of fertilization.[8] Much space was also given over to the treatment of various animal diseases. Less numerous but not unimportant were the contributions on chickens,[9] bees,[10] geese,[11] turkeys,[12] and hogs;[13] on Indian corn,[14] barley,[15] hay,[16] potatoes,[17] and hemp;[18] and, finally, on the draining of swamps.[19] These particulars represented the main agricultural interests and problems of the farmers of New York and the neighboring colonies.

While the almanac was trying to help the farmer make a better living out of the soil, it did not forget that his wife was engaged in an equally hard struggle—providing a home for his family. There was very little money with which to buy things, and the few possessions that had been inherited or had been added in the course of the years had to go a long way. Moreover, the various needs of the home somehow had to be derived from what the farm could produce. The task was not easy, requiring ingenuity and knowledge often beyond the reach of the husband and wife. The almanac could help them—and did. First came the paragraphs or articles which informed the housewife how, with the materials which were generally available on the farm, she could make her home more comfortable and pleasant: how to get rid of such pests as bugs, fleas, flies, mice, and rats;[20] how to keep chimneys from smoking;[21] how to prepare a cheap cement for glass and china;[22] how to make starch without corn[23] and soap without boiling;[24] how to take out grease stains;[25] and so forth. Next came the culinary hints: how to make bread from potatoes or turnips when there was no wheat flour or cornmeal;[26] how to get coffee from acorns[27] and sugar from various products of the farm, such as white and red beets, carrots, parsnips, or apples;[28] how to preserve butter or meat in hot weather;[29] and, last, a host of recipes for cheap native alcoholic beverages: cider,[30] mead,[31] wine,[32] and whiskey.[33]

Some of the suggestions, however, seem to have been offered with tongue in cheek. For example, *Thomas More* in his almanac for 1750 recommended this method of keeping the birds away from fruit trees: "Hang a bundle of Garlick on a Branch of a Tree, . . . and they will not touch your Fruit." In the almanac for 1752, he set forth a shortcut to catch birds and foxes: "Soak such Grain as they love, in Brandy or Rum, and it will make them drunk, so that you may catch them."

The farmer's practical interest in astrology encouraged almanac-authors to introduce selections and summaries on the new facts and theories of the rapidly growing science of "natural astrology" or astronomy. The experiment seems to have been successful, for the almanacs continued to print interesting articles on this science throughout the century. The disputed Copernican theory, naturally, came in for much discussion. As a result, the almanacs offer important contemporary evidence of the extent to which the Copernican doctrine had gained acceptance outside of scientific circles. The Cambridge almanac for 1675 by J. Foster included "A brief Description of the Coelestial Orbs," which is one of the earliest popular presentations of the theory in this country. Foster declared that it had been wholly accepted by astronomers "in this latter age," but himself found two "Notable Objections" to it, first, "the Infallible Authority of the Holy Scriptures so often mentioning the Suns motion," and, second, the fact that "the fixt Stars do bear a Contrary Aspect." The New York almanac for 1723 by B. A. Philo-Astro, in an article which the author asserted was designed especially "for the Information of the unlearned," explained and defended the Copernican hypothesis but admitted that it did not yet have "the publick Stamp." The statement is confirmed by Samuel Sewall's careful comment on the whole question: "I think it inconvenient to assert such Problems," which reflects the unsettled state of public opinion in the matter.[34] The *Nathaniel Ames* almanac for 1734 is more emphatic, remarking that the theory was no longer disputed by any "Man of Sense," but that would still leave a great many in the Ptolemaic camp. Ames, moreover, sought to reconcile the conception of Copernicus with the infallible authority of the Scriptures by arguing that the story of Joshua and the sun was to be interpreted figuratively rather than literally. *Thomas More,* 1760, still found it advisable in an essay, "Of the Sun and Moon," to remark that the Ptolemaic concept had been abandoned by "the most eminent modern Astronomers, Mathematicians, and Philosophers"; and a series of questions and answers on popular topics of the day in the *New Jersey Almanack* for 1770 included one set concerning the two theories, which involved a pretty solution of the religious question at issue. The author arrived at the conclusion that the Copernican explanation was the more satisfactory, and one could not rationally suppose that "infinite Wisdom" would rather choose the less satisfactory theory. In view of this evidence, I doubt that the Copernican theory became an article of universal popular faith in this country earlier than the Revolution, but I believe it was taken for granted generally by well-educated laymen by the end of the first third of the century.

The discussion of this question, as we have seen, usually turned up as part of simple introductory lessons in astronomy. Simple, it is true, but they invited the reader to take his eyes off the ground and look up into the sky with curiosity and awe, after he had read about the overwhelming size and speed of the planets, or the spectacular interplay of planetary movement that produced an eclipse, [35] or the fixed stars, which were themselves great suns surrounded by planets on which, perhaps, creatures like us lived.[36] Here and there, we find one of these lessons in rhyming verse, easy to memorize if the reader wanted to have his information in a compact little package.[37] There were many references to comets, in which the reader would be interested through both wonder and fear. The belief that they, like eclipses, were portents of disaster had been inherited from the ancient world and was still widely held in the eighteenth century by the learned and the unlearned. William Whiston, a disciple of Newton, had advanced the theory that the passing of a comet had caused the Biblical Flood,[38] and the almanac of *B. A. Philo-Astro* for 1723, accepting this view, added that the same comet, when it passed the earth on its return from the sun, would consume the earth in flames. In the decade before the Revolution, the disastrous significance of comets began to be questioned. Were they distant planets which somehow had slipped away from their orbits?[39] Perhaps it was their function to supply vapors to the planets and thereby prevent them from drying up.[40] People were saying that the conflict between the colonies and the mother country had been foreshadowed by a recent comet. Why, asked *Roger More,* (1770) should we presume to take this as a warning intended only for us, and not also for the Russians, the Turks, or the Chinese? Indeed:

> The arrogating of it to so diminutive a Part of the World as the British Empire, shews only a Degree of Pride nearly equal to that of the Fly on the Coach Wheel.

The disaffection in the colonies had already gone pretty far, I would surmise, judging by this remarkably un-English outlook on the British Empire.

The same reasoning was being applied to the time-honored interpretation of the meaning of eclipses. When John Clapp, in his almanac for 1697, had had the temerity to assert that they had no influence on human events since they were the result of natural causes, Daniel Leeds took up the cudgels the following year in behalf of tradition and countered with the observation that death by poison was also the result of natural causes. The *Leeds* almanacs never departed from his position, although a sign of weakening toward the end may be seen in the defense of the old doctrine by Titan Leeds in 1737 on psychological grounds, in accordance with which he maintained that "Mercurial Persons" were strongly affected by eclipses. After 1750, ridicule frequently raised its head in the New York almanacs on the pages of the eclipses.

As the geocentric concept of the universe faded out of men's minds, the anthropomorphic bias of established religion weakened. In the earlier part of the century, certain phases of the new science had been frankly enlisted in the cause of religion. For instance, one almanac proclaimed that the "Tellescope has enlarged the boundaries of the Universe and made the works of God seem nobler and grander."[41] Granted, but in time He and His works became so noble and grand that men began to feel a little estranged from Him and lost the old warm feeling that His chief occupation was the running of this planet and their affairs. Of what importance were they in a universe infinite in time and space?

When we turn to the hygienic and medical features of the New York almanacs, we are back again on the utilitarian side of the fence. Here we note an interesting fact that is generally overlooked, namely, that the almanac was no less useful to the physician than to the farmer. Many of the receipts and articles could obviously be of service only to the medical practitioner, as, for instance, the extract from a treatise on inoculation against smallpox, printed in the *Hutchins* almanac for 1768, or the letters of Dr. Jacob Ogden of Long Island on the "sore throat distemper" (diphtheria) appearing in the same almanac a few years later.[42] Moreover, since medicine and astrology had not yet been divorced, the man of signs and the daily zodiacal notations were indispensable. The doctrine of the four humors and the practice of bleeding and purging, which were still generally followed by physicians, were hardly more helpful than aspects of astrological learning. A curious illustration of this fact is the diploma issued in 1758 by Dr. Christopher Witt of Germantown, Pennsylvania to his pupil, John Kaighin, of Hathfield, New Jersey, who, he certified, had received instruction "not only in medical science, as we understand it, but also in the astral sciences," and had learned

> the Arts and Mysteries of Chymistry, Physick, & the Astral Sciences, whereby to make a more perfect Discovery of the Hidden causes of more occult & uncommon Disseases, not so easily to be discovered by the Vulgar Practice.[43]

The temptation to charlatanry was great. In this country, notwithstanding the fact that only a little over 10 percent of all the practitioners of medicine had medical degrees as late as 1775,[44] conditions were better than in England.[45] The colonies cannot muster a name worthy of comparison with the brilliant Sir William Read, who began his career as a tailor. Being ambitious and alert, he published a volume on diseases of the eye, which he had paid someone to write for him, and then opened an office on the Strand, where he was so successful that he came to the attention of Queen Anne, who suffered from bad eyesight. Quite pleased with his services, she knighted him.

Among the various physical afflictions for which the New York almanacs offered cures, "consumption" (tuberculosis),[46] "Bloody Flux" (dysentery),[47] cancer,[48] gout,[49] ague,[50] "Stone in Bladder,"[51] gravel,[52] and rheumatism[53] turn up most often. In a second group, of less importance, may be placed a miscellaneous assortment of ailments including smallpox,[54] deafness,[55] dropsy,[56] coughs,[57] "sore throat distemper,"[58] pleurisy,[59] rabies,[60] and corns.[61]

Most of the prescriptions were printed without any indication of their source; some appeared to be taken from professional publications.[62] One almanac-author warned his readers that the nostrums which he recommended might not help them because the climate might "alter the Virtues which were found to be in those Things elsewhere."[63]

It is both entertaining and instructive to peruse these old medical recipes. Here is an almanac remedy for a cold that is probably still used in many homes:

> Take half a Pint of Penny Royal Water [a medicinal liquor derived from a species of mint], Two Ounces of Sugar Candy, beat fine, and dissolve, make it hot, and drink it going to bed.[64]

A most astonishing cure for gout or rheumatism will be found in the *Freeman* almanac for 1768. The instructions are briefly these: Dig a hole in the ground four feet long, two and a half feet wide, and three feet deep, and then keep a fire burning in it for two hours. After the hole has cooled off, place the patient, wearing shirt and trousers, on a chair in the hole, his feet on a board, and cover the hole with blankets so as to leave only his head exposed. He is to remain there for one hour, during which he drinks four cups of snakeroot tea. At the end of the hour, wrap him in the blankets and put him back in bed. Continue to give him snakeroot tea once or twice every hour, and repeat the hole treatment once every other day until he has recovered. On the other hand, if one had tuberculosis, he merely ate a bunch of white grapes three times a day, fasted for one hour after each, and drank a glass of water before going to bed.[65] Or suppose one were bald before his time. *Hutchins,* 1770, advised: "Rub the part morning and evening with onions, 'till it is red; and rub it afterwards with honey." A none too fragrant ointment; still, a great improvement on some of the nauseating concoctions imposed on the colonists during the previous century. For example, a salve for bruises recommended in *Extracts from the Book of Phisick of William Penn*[66] consisted of a mixture of six pounds of butter, a bottle of black snails, a large oyster shell of cow dung, half as much fresh hen dung, and rosemary, lavender, elder, frankincense, and other esoteric ingredients!

There was probably very little difference between the medical receipts and the advertised patent medicines of the New York almanacs. If there was, it pertained to economics and psychology: The advertised stuff was more expensive and looked more impressive in a colored bottle with a seductive label. However, we should remember that an eighteenth-century patent medicine was no more of a fraud than an eighteenth-century physician—and did no more harm. The patent medicines of the almanacs, being *bona fide* representatives of their class, pretended to be good for almost anything that ailed the reader. Take, for example, "Doctor Watkinson's famous Family Medicine" advertised in the *Hutchins* almanac for 1769 by its printer, Hugh Gaine. In children it cured "Habitual Costiveness, Whooping Cough, Convulsions, Worms, breeding of Teeth, Gripings with green Stools, Eruptions, with all kinds of Swellings"; in adults, "Jaundice, Dropsy, Cholick, Scurvy, Obstructions, . . . Pain at the Stomach, &c." A similar faith animated the makers of "The poor Man's Medicine,"[67] "Turlington's Balsam of Life,"[68] and "Essence of the Balm of Gilead,"[69] and was undoubtedly transmitted to many readers.

The general advice on health, of which there was a great deal in the New York almanacs, seems very sensible and useful by contrast. Indeed, the modern reader, versed in the health fads of the twentieth century, will be surprised to find numerous suggestions regarding bathing, fresh air, diet, and the use of medicine that imply a substantial knowledge of proper hygiene as it is conceived today. The cardinal principle of health was held to be moderation, particularly in eating and drinking, and there is hardly an issue of a New York almanac that does not refer to or elaborate on this theme in prose or verse. A typical instance is the article on longevity which *Hutchins* for 1768 abstracted from Baron Haller's *Elements of Physiology*. Haller believed, although he stressed the importance of heredity, that every man could add years to his life by observing moderation in diet, bodily exercise, study, and "venery," in fact, in everything but sleep and "ambulation." And when one reads that buttermilk is an excellent restorative for "broken Constitutions," or that a proper diet should include plenty of vegetables,[70] he forgets for a moment that he is reading an old almanac of two hundred years ago and thinks he is reading a recent "physical culture" magazine.

On the whole, the medical and hygienic information intended for the instruction of the general reader stands the test of time much better than the portions of the medical "science" of the age provided for the use of the physician. The science, however, unless one thinks of the possible effects on the sick, makes better reading today: for example, old Daniel Leeds holding forth on the position of the moon in the signs in relation to the best time for bleeding, purging, and applying a "Plaister,"[71] or giving the "most apt Times to gather Herbs when the Planets that govern are dignified;"[72] his son Titan, expatiating on the "four Principal Humours";[73] or William Birkett commenting learnedly on the diseases incident to the seasons:

> The wish'd for and welcome Spring Quarter is naturally Hot and Moist, in nature of . . . [Jupiter], but if it so vary from its natural Temper, as being Windy and Dry, then it is, bad for antient People & Child-bearing Women; If very Wet; then expect dangerous Diseases, and Fever and Agues the Summer following, but if very cold and many south-East Winds & Fogs, then it is likely to breed Infectious Diseases.[74]

One of the most curious pieces of medical reading in the New York almanacs is a long article in *Roger More* for 1761: "Of the Cure of Wounds, &c. in The Magnetical Way," a theory widely discussed in the seventeenth century and still of great interest in the eighteenth. In 1698, for instance, it was the subject of a master's thesis in Harvard College.[75] In the words of *Roger More:*

> Take Roman Hungarian Vitriol, and dissolve it in common water, in a glass jar. Put therein any linen, or other thing stained with the blood of a wound, and let it lie for the vitriol to work upon the blood. Though the patient be at the distance of many miles, it will attract the corruption of his wounds, and stay the bleeding of

> them . . . . No other surgery is required for the patient, than keeping of the wound clean, and closing it up from the air.

The method was said to have been introduced in England by Sir Kenelme Digby in the early part of the seventeenth century and to have come to the attention of King James when one of his favorites was miraculously cured by Digby. Digby told the king he had learned the secret from a friend, who had received it from a Carmelite friar. The article cited several other cases of "magnetical" cures, such as the disappearance of warts after a piece of bacon with which they had been rubbed was nailed up on a window facing south and the improvement of patients in whom sweating, vomiting, or purging had been induced "magnetically" by mixing an unnamed substance with their wine. The article mentioned another substance "of magnetic virtue," "Persicaria Maculata," popularly known as "Arsesmart," to be used as follows:

> Beat it into a pulp, and lay it on a sore or ulcer, till it grow warm on the part; then take it off and bury it in a dunghill, and as it corrupts, the sore will heal.

During the greater part of the Bradford era, the astrological pretensions of the almanacs were rarely subjected to the skepticism and ridicule which had found expression in satirical almanacs. Convivial John Clapp might question the influence of eclipses, but readers continued to trust the weather predictions, consult the signs before planting and reaping or during sickness, and view eclipses and comets with trepidation. The advent of *Poor Richard* marked a new departure, from which neither *Titan Leeds* nor astrology ever quite recovered. In fact, the first unmistakable sign of the change appeared in Titan Leeds's own almanac for 1735 in a verse selection satirizing the claims of astrologers, according to whom

> There's but the twinkling of a Star
> Between a Man of Piece and War;
> A Thief and Justice, Fool and Knave,
> A huffing officer and slave;
> A crafty Lawyer and Pickpocket,
> A great Philosopher and Block-head;
> A formal Preacher and a Player,
> A learn'd Physician and Man-slayer:
> As if Men from the Stars did suck
> Old Age, Diseases, and ill Luck;
> Wit, Folly, Honour, Virtue, Vice,
> Trade, Travel, Women, Claps and Dice:

> And draw with the first Air they breathe,
> Battel and Murther, sudden Death.

After the end of the Leeds dynasty, the rationalist infection spread more rapidly. The time was ripe for it, witness shrewd Nathaniel Ames, in New England, analyzing the old superstition of witchcraft in the dry light of reason:

> If there be an old Woman . . . prodigious ugly, her Eyes hollow and red, her Face shrivel'd up, that goes double, and her Voice trembles, she is a Witch forsooth; but the handsome young Girls are never suspected; as tho' Satan took a Delight in the Dry Sticks of Humane Nature . . . .[76]

In New York the new trend could be observed most clearly in the *Copernicus* almanacs printed by Henry De Foreest,[77] but it was also apparent in those of *Thomas More*[78] and *W. Jones*.[79] One line of attack, as illustrated by the the selection in *Titan Leeds*, 1735, used satirical verse. The lusty verses in *Copernicus* for 1746 entitled "A Memento to Rakes, or a New Commentary upon the Old Twelve Signs," followed this method. A second employed the "receipt" device, for example, to make an "ass-trologer," one took four ounces of ignorance and superstition, mixed them with large quantities of vainglory, self-conceit, folly, impudence, and "Bambast Nonsense," and rolled the compound into pills, which were to be taken annually for ten years on the first of April in the early morning.[80]

Only one voice was raised in behalf of the "astral science," that of *Hutchins*, who severely upbraided all those "whose thick sculls can't penetrate into any Thing above the Earth; or out of the Reach of their Nose—Yet are so wise as to call those Arts they know nothing of sinful, diabolical, whimsical, and what not."[81] But it was fashionable to ridicule the stargazers, and they were scorned on every side.

In the meantime, nevertheless, the squat figure of the man of signs appeared in every almanac issue, and the calendar pages retained their astral notations for each day and their judiciously placed weather predictions. Some of the readers, it would seem, still used them, and the almanac-authors dared not openly discontinue a feature which they obviously considered a fraud. It remained for John Holt, the revolutionary printer, to find out to what extent they had underestimated the strength of the popular belief in astrology, which has recently manifested itself again. The preface to the first issue of his *Freeman* almanac (1767) contained the first frank denial of the value of the signs and weather predictions that appeared in a New York almanac. The author there remarked that the theory of the signs was obsolete and boldly asserted that its persistence in the almanacs was an insult to the intelligence of the readers. He had, therefore, "ventured to go out of the common Road" by treating his readers as "reasonable Creatures" and leaving out the signs and predictions. The response was unequivocal. *Freeman* sold poorly. The next issue, consequently, reverted to the tradition of insulting the intelligence of readers, but the 1769 number again challenged their intelligence by describing how dice were used to prepare the weather forecasts. The armed truce between author and reader lasted for a few more years and then, of necessity, collapsed. The *Freeman* almanac did not appear after 1772. Freeman and Holt perhaps had learned that people cling to myths that make them feel better.

CHAPTER 8

Literature for Settlement and Frontier

The didactic spirit of the eighteenth century and the didactic function of the almanac are strikingly reflected in the verse and prose of the New York almanacs. With the exception of the calendar verse celebrating the months and seasons, the reading matter is predominantly instructive. Even those pieces which seem designed mainly for the entertainment of the reader frequently betray the didactic motive in their satiric tone.

The literary supplement of the almanacs was an outgrowth of the short selections in verse or prose which were first introduced on the calendar pages, usually at the top, to fill out the page usefully. *Daniel Leeds*, for example, presented a little article on medicinal herbs in this manner.[1] When less practical literary fare was included, some readers apparently felt that they were not getting their money's worth, and in the almanac for 1718 we find *Titan Leeds* asking the readers to let him know what their preferences were, and carefully eschewing verse for three years until "vox populi" was made clear. The reappearance of verse in the almanac for 1722 proclaimed that the almanac had been made safe for literature.

On the other hand, the nonacademic background of most of the readers was responsible for the general indifference of almanac-authors, and, presumably, of readers, to the literary quality of the selections and, consequently, to their authorship or source. The choice fruits of books, magazines, newspapers, and almanacs were freely culled without acknowledgment, and numerous original contributions were printed anonymously. Many an "inglorious Milton" of Colonial America rests peacefully in the dusty pages of the almanacs.

If the modern reader finds most of the verse and prose in the New York almanacs mediocre in thought and expression, let him, before passing judgment, recall that the ideas which seem commonplace and the phrases which seem stale to him undoubtedly had novelty and freshness for readers who were unfamiliar with the literature of their own time and of preceding ages. To Colonial folk, cut off from newspapers, magazines, and books, and from easy communication with neighbors, the literary glimpses afforded by the annual almanac, however limited these might be, afforded discoveries and delights that can no longer be enjoyed by the surfeited reader of the present. The selections, moreover, represented a degree of literary proficiency well above the popular level, even if we disregard the not infrequent specimens of the work of such writers as Shakespeare, Milton, Swift, Pope, and Voltaire. The almanac, no less than the Bible, served to mold and improve the spoken and written language of the common people.

Viewed chronologically, the authors who happened to break through the net of anonymity cast over most of the excerpts in the New York almanacs indirectly measure the rising and widening tide of popular culture during the century, the expanding of the intellectual universe of the common people, and the developing and refining of popular taste and appreciation. The Bradford period (1694–1744) yielded very few names: Bacon,[2] Dryden,[3] Richard Blackmore,[4] and Vergil.[5] Pope was fleeced without attribution.[6] During the period of expansion (1745–1776), however, he came into his reward,[7] and was joined by a goodly company: Gower[8] Shakespeare,[9] Milton,[10] Addison,[11] Swift,[12] the *Spectator,*[13] Smollett,[14] Voltaire,[15] Juvenal,[16] and Marcus Aurelius.[17] Such studies as have been made of the almanacs printed in the other colonies tell a similar story.[18]

Verse

Those who have occasion to read a great deal of almanac verse should keep in mind what that canny old Yankee Nathaniel Ames once told his readers about the verses in his own almanacs: "I desire you would be pleased to take them as some men take their wives, for better or for worse," and I might add that at times this comparison between verses and wives seems uncomfortably accurate. The quality of almanac verse, it would seem, continued to be conditioned to a certain extent by its original use as a means of filling up surplus space, as *Poor Robin* of Newport aptly stated:

> Had not my muse drunk ale in plenty
> This vacancy must have been empty.[19]

Long after the practical origin of almanac verse had been forgotten, the matter of space still operated as a limitation. Note this statement in the *Old Farmer's Almanac* for 1822 to one of the contributors: "We

should have been better pleased if the lines had contained less sylla-
bles, eight is the utmost we are able to get into a line—have reserved
it for our next."[20]

The almanac-author felt free, of course to take his verse selections from any available source, not omitting the productions of his
brother philomaths. For example, the calendar verses for March, July,
and September in the *Thomas More* almanac for 1749 are found in
Titan Leeds for 1744. A piece beginning: "The Fields that were with
Scarlet Flow'rs o'er-spread," which first was printed in *Titan Leeds*,
1731, turned up several times during the century.[21] Another favorite
is the epigrammatic "Our Life is nothing but a Winter's day."[22]

In borrowing material, the almanac-author did not scruple to assume the eighteenth-century privilege of adaptation, of which there
are many interesting examples. For instance, the calendar verses for
June in *Titan Leeds* for 1733 are a synthesis of the following lines in
Pope's *Essay on Criticism*: 412, 413, 430–433, 436, and 437, which incidentally illustrates the difficulty of using the Pope couplet to make a
chain of interlinked parts. Too often his couplets form a string of
beads, beautifully polished, but interchangeable. Again, Shakespeare's

> Neither a borrower, nor a lender be;
> For loan oft loses both itself and friend,
> And borrowing dulls the edge of husbandry

undergoes this pedestrian alteration:

> Neither a Borrower nor a Lender be,
> For Borrowing dulls the Edge of Industry;
> The Lender often loseth his best Friends,
> And Interest seldom answers both their Ends.

A more curious product is a poem in the *Felix Leeds* almanac for 1727,
entitled "On Wit," which, upon closer inspection, turns out to be
largely a patchwork of odds and ends from Pope's *Essay on Criticism*
and Dryden's *Absalom and Achitophel*.

A good part of the verse in the almanacs is heavy-footed and re-
miniscent of the pseudopoetic crutches supplied to the schoolboy at
that time in his *Gradus ad Parnassum* to help him compose Latin verse.
It is not, however, much inferior to the magazine verse of that century, and generally better than the verse in the contemporary English
almanacs.[23] But let the defendant speak for himself: the following
complete set of calendar verses from *Titan Leeds*, 1740 is fairly typical:

January

Man's subject to Accidents, and born in strife
'Twixt Joy and Pain we pass a restless Life;
More Grief than Pleasure, in all Stations find,
And own at last, that Sorrow rules Mankind,
Thus Man forever Labours, and Decays;
In Tiresome Night, he wearies out his Days,
He scarce a minute Glories in his bloom,
So nigh, alas! The Cradle and the Tomb.

February

The Storms that in a milder Moon were bred
Now burst their Ways, and fill the World with Dread;
The furious Winds in every quarter Roar,
And threatning Bellows Ches'peek Shore.
Stand by good Jack lower your Yards amain,
When this is past, it will be fair again.

March

When Sol thro Aries drives his brilliant Car,
And hostile Bosoms kindle for the War;
When softer Souls the sweeter Pleasures rove,
And melt in Raptures the Idalian Love;
When blooming Nature to the Eye displays
Its pleasing Pride a thousand thousand Ways,
Then longing Mortals with impatience wait,
For my approach, which is as sure as Fate.

April

The promise now of Halcyon Days is seen,
Between a Jovial Youth and lovely Queen;
Not on Saint-George's Day, which none e'er knew,
On what fair Ground the Saint or Dragon grew;
Yet some do make of it a holy Day,
For Sots to Tipple, or for Maids to play.

May

Wellcome thou Blume of Spring, returning May,
Attendant Beauty still adorns thy sway;
From thee around, unnumbered Blessings flow,
And picture Heav'n on glad'ning Worlds below.
While Nature pays with Praise, I fain would bring
My nimble Reed, and what I owe thee, sing;
But since my Musick can but rudely flow,
May must still trust me for what I owe.

June

In spring let loose thy Males, then all things prove
The Stings of Pleasure, and the Pangs of Love,
Aetherial Jove then glads with geneal Show'rs
Earths mighty Womb, and strows her Lap with Flow'rs.
Hence Juices mount, and Buds embolden'd, try
More kindly Breezes, and a softer Sky;
Kind Venus revels, hark! On every Bow
In lulling strains, the feather'd Warblers Woo.

July

When scorch'd with summer's sultry Heat we burn,
The cooling Breezes refresh in their Return;
When tir'd with th' Toils and Labours of the day,
We bless the wish'd for Evening's milder Ray.
Around the Board we quaff the social Bowl
With Indies gen'rous Liquor we Regale the Soul,
Its Heat, pure Water's gentle Pow'r Restrains,
And cools the raging Thirst which parch'd our Veins.

August

All Nature smiles. Come now, nor fear my Love
To taste the Odours of the Wood-bine Grove,
And pass the Evening Glooms in harmless Play,
And sweetly steering, languish Life away;
An Altar bound with recent Flowers, I rear
To thee, best Season of the various Year.
All hail! Such days in beautious Order ran,
So sweet, so soft, when first the World began.

September

In Eden's Bowers, when Man's great Sire assign'd
The Names and Nature of the brutal Kind,
Then Lamb and Lyon friendly walk'd their Round,
And Hare, undaunted, lick't the fondling Hound.
Wondrous to tell! But when with luckless Hand,
Our darling Mother broke the Sole Command;
Then Want and Envy brought their meagre Train,
Then Death came down, and Death had leave to reign.

October

A Soul which uncorrupted Nature sways,
With calm indifferent Fortune's gift surveys;
If Providence an affluent Store denys,
Its own intrinsick Worth that want supplys;

Disdains by Vicious Actions to acquire
That glitt'ring Trifle vulgar Minds admire,
With ease to Heav'ns superior will resigns,
Nor meanly at anothers Wealth repines.

November

What-e'er we think on't Fortune's but a Toy,
Which cheats the Soul with empty Shows of Joy;
A meer ideal Creature of the Brain
That rules the Idol of the Mad and Vain;
Deludes their Senses with a fair Disguise,
And sets Airial Bliss before their Eyes;
But when they hope to grasp the glittering Prey,
The instable Fantom vanishes away.

December

Man by necessity compell'd, must go
O'er Rocks of Peril, and thro' Vales of Wo.
Man with the Morn, begins his destin'd Race,
Joy in his Eye, and Pleasure in his Face.
But oh! What rubs attend his setting Days;
His Sinnews slacken, and his Strength decays;
His weak Limbs ake, with hourly Toil opprest,
Till wish'd for Night restores him peaceful Rest.

As these selections show, the heroic couplet was the popular verse form. During the early part of the century, it was the only form employed, outside of a few examples of the tetrameter couplet and the pentameter line in different rhyme arrangements. Unrhymed verse did not appear until midcentury, and thereafter quite infrequently. After 1750, the tetrameter couplet increased in popularity, finally drawing up almost on a par with the heroic couplet.

Hardly any kind of writing escaped the rhyming fashion. Even land purchase laws were cast in rhyme, and seemed so "sweetly sung" to the almanac-author that he made known his intention to turn *Cook's Institutes* and all the province laws into rhyme, "hoping thereby to engage some of our young Lawyers and old Justices to read a little."[24]

The verse of the New York almanacs falls into four main classes—didactic, descriptive, humorous, and lyrical, the first being predominant, and the first and second including most of the verse. The range of quality is great in all four classes, with most of the selections within the lower half of the literary scale. At one end there is a masterpiece of desiccation, like Frederick the Great's *The Relaxation of War: or the Hero's Philosophy*, which opens with the royal lines:

> Love by hope is still sustain'd,
> Zeal by the reward that's gained,
> In pow'r authority begins,
> Weakness strength from prudence wins."[25]

At the other end one comes upon this echo of Hadrian's celebrated "Animula":

> Why art thou, little Life, so often crost,
> So seldom pleasing, and so easy lost?
> So restless, teazing, and so very vain,
> I'm sick, then leave me, life, yield up thy slave,
> Yield me to death, and to the peaceful grave,
> Where sorrows cease, where fears and troubles cease,
> Where knaves are silent, and where fools have peace.[26]

And the rousing hymn:

> God several ways Mens hearts hath Try'd,
> He fools their Wits and shames their Pride,
> And by their shame is glorifi'd
>   Sing therefore Hallelujah.
> To Tryal every Man he brings.
> He spares not Commoners nor Kings,
> And of his Deeds the whole Earth rings
>   Sing therefore Hallelujah.
> He wounds, he cures, he builds and breaks,
> He kills and saves, he gives and takes,
> As he finds cause, he marrs and makes,
>   Sing therefore Hallelujah.
> He by contention endeth Strife
> By leaving helpless gives Relief,
> And by Death bringeth unto Life.
>   Sing therefore Hallelujah.
> As he fore-told us heretofore,
> Revenge pursues the Scarlet Whore
> And she ere long shall be no more
>   Sing therefore Hallelujah.[27]

Much of the didactic verse in the New York almanacs was of a satirical nature, and, in the true manner of eighteenth-century satire, often caustic and coarse. The coarseness however, was not confined to the satirical verse, as we have observed, nor to the New York almanacs, for the tradition of Rabelais was carried on conscientiously in the best American almanacs of the eighteenth century, such as *Hutch-*

ins, *Ames*, and *Poor Richard*. The descriptive verse was limited mostly to the calendar poems dedicated to the months and seasons. A good deal of it, like the same verse in the contemporary English almanacs, was conventional and artificial, relying more on classical imagery than reality, but some of it, however crude, indicates that attempts were being made to represent the American landscape, particularly the winter scene:

> Winter with his cold Breath doth glaze the Floods,
> And purls with Frosts the Fields and naked Woods.
> Next months the Snow doth make the Fields look old,
> And many Men turn Quakers with the Cold.[28]

Much of the almanac verse, particularly the humorous, is characterized by a homely and colloquial style that is not unattractive, as the following selection, "The Rib," demonstrates:

> Adam alone could not be easy,
> So he must have a wife, an't please you:
> But did he procure his wife,
> To cheer his solitary life?
> Why from a rib cut off his side
> Was form'd this necessary bride.
> But how did he the pain beguile?
> Pho! he slept sweetly all the while,
> But when this rib was reapplied,
> In woman's form to Adam's side,
> How then, I pray you, did it answer?
> He never slept so sweet again, Sir.

This style is in striking contrast to that of a large number of selections appearing in the latter half of the century which mark the ascendance of the cult of sensibility:

> Ye that have passions for a tear,
> Give nature vent, and drop it here.[29]

Tears flowed, however, only in appropriate settings—shaded woods, cypress groves, and country churchyards. The theme of unhappy love flourished, and the Edwins and Emmas, the Davids and Delias of the age suffered in a heartless world, and wept, and sometimes died of pining.[30] The new humanitarianism also provided a welcome opportunity for lacrimal irrigation, stimulating such gushings as:

> Ah me! how little knows the human heart
> The pleasing task of soft'ning others woe,

Stranger to joys that pity can impart,
And tears sweet sympathy can teach to flow!
If e'er I've mourned my humble, lowly state,
If e'er I've bowed my knee at Fortune's shrine,
If e'er a wish escap'd me to be great,
The fervent Pray'r, Humanity, was thine.

There is hardly an important feature of contemporary life and thought which the verse of the New York almanacs did not at one time or another touch upon. The current ideas and movements in science, religion, economics, politics, and morality were presented in verse as well as in prose—a fact which contributed greatly to its educative value. Many of the topics treated in verse have already been taken up in preceding chapters, as, for instance, matters of health and hygiene, moral views, and religius questions. Then there is a large body of verse expounding the traditional social sentiments on a wide variety of abstractions and qualities such as justice, fortune, industry, envy, friendship, happiness, and the like. The following lines on fortune are representative of this class:

Very powerful is the pur-blind witch
To raise up Knaves, and make Fools Devilish Rich,
To set an Ass on top of all her Wheel,
And to kick Vertue backward with her Heel,
To raise a Pedler, Pander, or a Jester,
And therefore hang the Hag, I do detest her.[31]

Life, death, and nature, in particular, were constantly recurring themes, partly because of their appropriateness in a book designed to simplify man's relation to the world of time and space and partly because of the prevailing literary taste for these subjects. Comments on these subjects appear very early in calendars and almanacs, as in the *Kalendar of Shepherdes,* for example, at the beginning of the sixteenth century.[32] The contemporary evidence may be seen in Young's very popular *Night-Thoughts,* which are grouped under the headings of life, death, immortality, time, friendship, virtue, and truth.

The comments on life dwelt chiefly on two aspects, the inexorable advance of time[33] and the general futility and miserableness of existence on this planet.[34] The passing of time was a favorite theme of the almanac versifiers, and utilized such stock figures as the burning candle, the passing day, and the revolving seasons. A good example of the type is the version of Simon Wastell's poem, "Of Man's Mortality," which was printed anonymously in the *Freeman* almanac for 1769 under the title, "On The Shortness of Human Life." The first few lines go:

> Like to the damask rose you see,
> Or like a blossom on a tree,
> Or like a dainty flower of May,
> Or like the morning to the day,
> Or like the sun, or like the shade,
> Or like the gourd which Jonas had,
> E'en such is man;—whose thread is spun,
> Drawn out, and cut, and so is done.—
> The rose withers, the blossom blasteth,
> The flower fades, the morning hasteth,
> The sun sets, the shadow flies,
> The gourd consumes,—the man he dies.

The mortuary verse presented familiar concepts. Most of it consists of variations on the idea that life's a stage, and death rings down the curtain; since the former is none too pleasant, and the latter inevitable, we should face the end calmly, especially if we have lived virtuous lives. Very few of the later poems, however, were founded on the fear of punishment after death. That was apparently waning, but a new fear, born of the skepticism induced by the classical Renascence and modern science, was taking its place—the possibility of total annihilation of personality by death. To counteract this, the almanacs could do little more than counsel the good life and the brave bearing. The good man, as one poem affirms in words that roughly prefigure the final scene of Bryant's *Thanatopsis*,

> . . . when Death calls, no Weakness does betray,
> Nor to an unbecoming Fear gives way;
> But to himself, and to his Maxims true,
> Lies smiling down and bids the world adieu.[35]

The influence of science was also felt in some of the verse devoted to nature. A part of this was merely expository, setting forth a few of the most notable discoveries of science. In this group belong the numerous metrical lessons in astronomy. These were poems expressing the wonder and awe of man in contemplating the grandeur and order of the physical universe.

The verse in the New York almanacs may be divided into two parts, according to the attitude expressed toward life. The first and larger part regarded life as a serious matter spent in the shadow of death. One is reminded of the old-time elementary classroom in reading these poems—with the wisdom of the ages set forth in aphorisms posted high on the walls while out in front the earnest schoolmistress frequently reviews the elevated moral sentiments until they have been learned by heart. The second part is quite different, rather like a marketplace. Here life is presented as a spectacle full of incongruity, chicanery, pretension, and folly, not to be taken too seriously. Raucous laughter is often heard. Laughter may avail where indignation fails. One makes the best of things, enjoys as many of the good things of this world as he can. If he is kicked, he grins and gets out of the way next time. The people in these verses are not as refined and well educated as the personages in the first part. They are boisterous, outspoken, unpolished, but less anemic.

Prose

The transition from verse to prose in the literature of the New York almanacs does not involve a radical change since there was little real difference in style, content, and point of view between the two kinds of writing. Both generally employed a fairly similar manner of expression, dealt with a great variety of similar topics, and sought to instruct and entertain the reader. Most of the prose items, like those in verse, were appropriated from other published sources, the only important exception being the annual prefaces, which were original and therefore all the more interesting.

Daniel Leeds had made them a regular feature of his almanac and had established in them a liveliness and informality of style which most of his successors wisely followed. They were used by him and other almanac-authors for explanation and discussion and at times took on the character of a modern editorial. They contained humorous comments on contemporary events, remarks on religious, economic, and political questions, disputes with competing almanac-authors, and, in times of war and revolution, patriotic or factional appeals which must have swayed the readers profoundly in those years of isolation. Inasmuch as many of these prefaces are examined in the next chapter, I shall limit myself here to a pair of typical specimens. The first is from the preface to the *Copernicus* almanac for 1746:

> To any Reader in the Pack,
> Who buys or reads my Almanack,
> All you that only one will try,
> Read, or not Read, be sure to buy.

> I Once more send my Predictions amongst you, which tho' written in a merry style, I dare presume Mirth and Truth walk together Hand in Hand; Read if you like and judge as you list, please yourselves and I am pleas'd, (in a word) I beg your Favour, crave your Acceptance, intreat your Kindness, implore your Love, request your Friendship. Homer and Virgel had both of them their Detractors; what then! If an Ass kick us, we must not

put him into the Court nor swear the peace against him and bind him over to the Sessions. Some gall'd Jades may perhaps wince at somewhat is here written. I protest I have no intent to expose any particular person, if they learn to know themselves I have my Wish, but if they snarl, 'tis a thousand Pound to a Nutshell they are the Persons hinted at. If therefore you are wise, make no wry Mouths at it, lest by that means you chance to be detected . . . .

The other is from the *Thomas More* almanac for 1748:

I guess without pretending to Infallibility, that if this War continues long, Man will grow something scarcer than they are; and it being Leap-Year, Maidenheads will be cried about like Oysters, to the great accomodation of those pretty Fellows, who don't care to venture their Carcasses with Mars, but rather stay at Home with Venus, purely to take care of the Breed; tho' notwithstanding this Scarcity of Men, some Fair-One's will carry a crack'd Utensil to their Bridal-Bed, which will make their Dearee's scratch their Heads, where they find the Flaw too staring. But if all Husbands, to whom the like Adventure has happened, shou'd be tempted to hang themselves, good gentle Reader, consider whether you have nothing of that Sort to fear for yourself.

The "observations" on the months and seasons included in several New York almanacs resembled these excerpts in style and spirit. These "observations" were a regular feature of the ribald satirical almanacs published in England during the seventeenth and eighteenth centuries, particularly *Poor Robin,* and resemble the satirical remarks in Rabelais's "prognostication" for 1532. One can, therefore, appreciate the annoyance of the respectable Roger Sherman upon discovering that a series of them had been inserted in his almanac for 1750 by the printer, De Foreest, without his permission. Other almanac-authors did not, however, share Sherman's dislike for them, for similar pieces appeared several times after his public denunciation of them in the *New York Gazette.*[36]

The rest of the prose literature divides itself largely into three groups: tales and stories, essays, and proverbs. Because of the limited size of the almanac, these usually had to be presented in abbreviated form, and often bear the impress of the almanac-author's literary skill and judgment, or lack of them. The style of most of the items is conventional, and the intent markedly didactic. The line between the first two groups was not always clearly drawn. There is so much moralizing in the short narratives and so much anecdote in the essays that it is sometimes difficult to decide in which category to place a given piece.

The most obviously didactic of the stories were anecdotes and fables. The former were mainly of the Plutarchian variety, illustrating moral virtues, the essence of which was compressed into a memorable utterance.[37] For example, Chiomata, the wife of Orthiagon, after being ransomed in Rome, had one of the Roman tribunes assassinated. When she brought his head to her husband, he was perturbed by the offering and asked her whether she did not regard the act as inconsistent with honor. She replied: "I do, but still I think it more consistent with my Honour and Reputation that of all the Men ever concerned with me there is but one alive."[38] This worthy sentiment inspired the sensible almanac-author to remark that Chiomata may have been less "romantically virtuous" than Lucretia but was "more prudent in attesting her Modesty, rather by the Death of her Ravisher than her own."

Another common type of story in the later New York almanacs was the moralistic Oriental tale or romance, a literary form which was very much in fashion at that time on both sides of the Atlantic.[39] The almanac versions, however, are Oriental in barely more than the names of the characters, being essentially expanded variations of the Plutarchian anecdote, with the same emphasis on a specific virtue and the same quotable climax. The novelty consisted in the more ornate trappings.

The phenomenon of sleepwalking, a very popular subject of discussion in the second half of the century, offered writers a novel modification of the immemorial dream-device. The New York almanacs treated the subject seriously and facetiously, now marveling at this psychological curiosity, now utilizing its humorous possibilities. An instance of the humorous point of view is the "Comical Adventure of a Sleep-Walker," printed in *Hutchins* for 1776, which tells how sleepwalking led to matrimony. The young man, spending the night with a relative, was awakened at three o'clock in the morning by the entrance of his cousin clad only in her nightdress. She calmly poked the fire and then lay down in his bed. Being a gentleman, he waited to see what would happen. In a few minutes she arose and left his room. When he rashly told the story the following day, her father rose to the occasion and declared that "since his Daughter had already gone to Bed to his Kinsman, it should be his Fault if he did not go to Bed to his Daughter, he being willing to bestow her upon him, with a good Fortune." The young lady, being a dutiful daughter, raised no objections, and the marriage was soon solemnized.

Other subjects of frequent occurrence were the mutability of fortune, the loyal servant, the generous master, and the miser. The first subject often took the form of showing how fortune humbled the pride of the rich belle who had rejected the impecunious suitor merely because he could not support her in proper style. Sometimes, however, the suitor became rich, found the once proud lady pitifully indigent and chastened, and frustrated poetic justice by marrying her.[40]

The essays were mainly in the line of the Bacon tradition rather than that of the *Spectator*, emphasizing sententiousness instead of character. They moralized on matters of sex and religion, personal virtues and vices, happiness, and the business of earning a livelihood. The last subject received a great deal of attention. Readers were constantly impressed with the importance of being solvent and having a nest egg; and the ingredients of the formula recommended by the almanacs for achieving that end were honesty, industry, and frugality, undoubtedly a good formula for the American of the eighteenth century.[41]

Of all the literary forms appearing in the eighteenth-century almanac, the proverb proved to be the one best adapted to its format and aim. This was largely due to the fact that it could be easily accommodated to the limited space of the annual and the limited education of its readers, and, furthermore, provided a concise way of conveying instruction on any topic. The proverbs of *Poor Richard*, for various reasons, achieved a greater fame than those of other American almanac-authors, but they are essentially similar in expression and spirit to those printed, for instance, in the earlier *Leeds* almanacs and later in those of *Ames, Hutchins, More,* and the others—shrewd digests of experience expressed in the vernacular:

Love and the Cough cannot be hid.[42]

A Horse that kicks and a Woman that speaks Latin never come to a good end.[43]

The images were drawn from everyday life and reflected the familiar occupations of town and country.

Most of the proverbs, like the rest of the literary contents of the almanacs, were borrowed from available sources,[44] especially other almanacs; some were original; and a few were in Latin.[45] As they were arranged to fill in the blank spaces on the calendar pages, the reader often had to follow a devious path to reach the nugget of wisdom at the end of the trail, but he was usually repaid for his effort and probably enjoyed the search and the suspense.

The proverbs in the New York almanacs, in general, covered the same ground as the other literary forms. Religion occupied a relatively insignificant place and received mention principally as a source of strife and intolerance. The proverbs advanced a practical philosophy calculated to serve the small farmer, artisan, and tradesman and based on the assumption that health and wealth were the foundation of happiness. In accordance with this view, they persistently dwelt on the values of reticence, mistrust, moderation, industry, and frugality.

No amount of generalization and description can quite satisfactorily convey their full force and flavor, and no other single literary form brings back for us the ideas and interests of the common people of that century as concisely and intimately as they do. For these reasons, and also because there is no collection of the proverbs that appeared in the New York almanacs, I include the following representative selection.

Money

Winter spends what Summer lends.[46]
Penny & Penny Laid up will be many.[47]
What's gain'd o'er's back is spent under his belly.[48]
A small pack becomes a little Pedlar.[49]
Where Bread is wanting all's to be sold.[50]
Love can do much, Money can do all.[51]
There is no Lock but a Golden Key will open it.[52]
A Golden Fool will be respected, and the Poor Wise Man is
　　rejected.[53]
All Men like Money, some their Wives.[54]
Honesty is the best policy, but Knavery is most in Fashion.[55]

Health

More health is gotten by observing Diet,
　　Than pleasure found in vain Excess and Riot.[56]
Be moderate in thy Drink & Meat,
　　Eat to live, not live to eat.[57]
A good Stomach is the best sauce.[58]
Often drunk, and seldom sober,
　　Falls like the Leaves in October.[59]

Religion

Saints in the Church, but Goats in the Garden.[60]
'Tis not the Habit, but the Heart that makes a man
　　Religious.[61]
First worship God; he that forgets to pray bids not himself
　　good-morrow or good day.[62]

Education

The best horse needs breaking, And the aptest child needs
    teaching.[63]
Let parents plant; let tutors water; but let both look up to the
    Father of Spirits for the desired increase.[64]
Read the best Books, Hear the best Men, Mind the best
    Things, Do Justice to all.[65]

Law and Medicine

Physitian, cure thyself.[66]
The People's health is the Doctors sickness.[67]
The Jews spend money at Easter, the Moors at Marriages, and
    the Christians at Suits in Law.[68]
Lawyers and Priests with thee'l agree
    If unto both thou'lt give a Fee.[69]

Politics

A man that keeps steady to one party, tho' he happens to be
    in the wrong, is still an honest man.[70]
All parties blame persecution when they feel the smart on't,
    and all practise it when they have the rod in their own
    hands.[71]
A long reach and as little conscience are necessary
    qualifications to a minister of state as a long hand and
    little fingers are to a man-midwife.[72]
Scepters are as brittle as Reeds.[73]
Sudden power is apt to be insolent, Sudden liberty saucy.[74]

Women

Wedding and ill-wintering tames both Man & Beast.[75]
She that wears Cork't shoes will prove light-headed.[76]
Love me little, love me long."[77]
See how they intermarry, Hot June unto cold January.[78]
Chuse neither Women nor Linnin by candle light.[79]
A fair Maid with a good Dower is all the year a July Flower.[80]
Take my advice & go to Bed, and be content with whom
    thou'rt wed.[81]
Let not thy Horse drink at every Run, Nor thy Wife run to
    every Gossiping.[82]

Old Cloathes and old Wives are not much minded.[83]
Honest men marry soon, Wise men not at all.[84]
He who marries for love without money, hath good nights
      and sorry days.[85]
A bad Wife and a back door.[86]
An Attorney with one Cause is not half so restless as a
      Woman with one Lover.[87]
He who sometimes goes astray, thinks his Wife goes the same
      way.[88]
A Wine-bibbing Dame and her Body yeilds [sic] to shame.[89]
The Old Woman would not seek her Daughter in the Oven,
      had she not been there herself.[90]

Old Favorites

Droping Water makes the stone hollow.[91]
When Fortune knocks, be sure to open the Door.[92]
Penny wise, pound foolish.[93]
March comes in like a Lyon, but goes out like a Lamb.[94]
The barking Dog bites little.[95]
Out of the Frying pan into the Fire.[96]
As mad as March Hare.[97]
Birds of a feather flock together.[98]
Better half a Loaf than no Bread.[99]
Strike while the Iron is Hot.[100]
It's an ill-wind that blows Nobody no Good.[101]
A rolling stone is ever bare of moss.[102]
Haste makes waste.[103]

General

Drive not too many Ploughs at once.[104]
He that is vain because he's wealthy, insults the sick because
      he's healthy.[105]
He that boasts his Ancestors, confesseth he has no Virtue of
      his own.[106]
Sober men conceal what drunken men reveal.[107]
A close Mouth catches no flyes.[108]
Day and Truth may be discerned thro' a little hole.[109]
Old Wine, an old Friend, and old Gold are beloved in all
      Places.[110]
Two ears and One Tongue suit well.[111]
Misers and Hogs are best picking when dead.[112]

He that once a good Name gets May p . . . the Bed, and say
    he Sweats.[113]
Some like Jonah in the Whale's Belly, travel much, and see
    little.[114]
Nothing humbler than Ambition, when it is about to climb.[115]
Mankind are very odd creatures; one-half censure what they
    practise, the other half practise what they censure, the
    rest always say and do as they ought.[116]
Old Boys have their Play things as well as young ones. The
    difference is only in the price.[117]
A dogmatical Tone, a pragmatical Pate.[118]
A Word to the Wise may make him wiser.[119]
Children are a certain Trouble; but an uncertain Pleasure.[120]
Time makes wrinkles in spite of the Leaden Fore-head
    Cloath.[121]

Summarizing, I would repeat that the Colonial almanac-authors, though not indifferent to literary quality, were primarily interested in entertainment and instruction. They did not generally bother to indicate the source or authorship of selections and freely adapted them to suit their own aims. From their point of view, form was subordinate to matter and purpose, but this view did not preclude their drawing on Shakespeare, Bacon, Milton, Dryden, Swift, Addison, Pope, Thomson, Voltaire, and Smollett, and it did not stop their readers from becoming acquainted with many literary types and styles, among which the prevailing influences went back to Bacon, LaFontaine, Dryden, Thomson, Pope, and Richardson.

The Colonial almanacs also served the cause of literature in America by providing an opportunity of anonymous publication to many local amateur writers. These original contributions were rarely above the level of mediocrity, but their appearance in print gave pleasure at least to their authors and on a small scale stimulated local literary activity as the small country newspapers of today do. In short, the almanacs, although primarily committed to dispensing such information, entertainment, and advice as the needs and preferences of their readers seemed to demand, provided them with an elementary literary education and an outlet for the exercise of literary talent, thereby playing a significant part in developing and defining American culture and literature.

CHAPTER 9

Nationality and Independence

The Declaration of Independence marked the beginning of American nationality and independence only to the extent that birth marks the beginning of life. From this point of view, the Declaration was also the culmination of a long period of prenatal development which dates, as John Adams once remarked, from the first plantation in America.[1] In studies of this period, the Colonial almanac of the eighteenth century has occasionally been mentioned as one of the cultural factors in the growth of American nationality and independence, but no thorough and systematic attempt has yet been made to examine this aspect of its history.

If we are to evaluate justly the importance of its contribution to the slow process whereby the different settlements widely dispersed throughout the wilderness along the Atlantic seaboard were finally welded into the United States of America, we should keep certain facts well in mind. In the first place, owing to the difficulties of travel and transporation, there was relatively little communication not only between colonies, but also between communities within each colony, until about the time of the war with France. Second, most of the people, either for lack of money or remoteness from the main centers and avenues of distribution, had no access to books, magazines, or newspapers. Third, during these years, the only periodical publication on contemporary events and ideas that had a general circulation was the almanac. Itinerant peddlers carried it to the most remote and isolated villages and farms; the most successful almanacs, such as *Leeds, Ames, Poor Richard,* and *Hutchins,* were sold far beyond the Colonial boundaries within which they were printed. For instance, answers to the "mathematical questions" proposed in the *Titan Leeds* almanac for 1731 were received from readers in New Jersey, Pennsylvania, and South Carolina. Moreover, the various almanacs, whether published in the same colony or different colonies, were similar in content and outlook, partly because they were intended for readers of the same degree of education and the same economic and social class, and partly because they imitated their most successful competitors. As a result, the instruction imparted by them on contemporary questions of economics, science, religion, morality, and politics generally supported the popular point of view, provided a common fund of knowledge and belief derived from the predominant interests of the age, and stimulated the creation of a public opinion knowing no Colonial barriers. Contributing to this result was the fact that the almanacs were subjected to very little direct censorship during this century.

For these reasons, then, the considerable measure of unity of thought and emotion which manifested itself when the conflict with the mother country came to a head must be credited in part to the continuous influence exerted by the almanac for three-quarters of a century preceding the clash. In the critical years before and after the Declaration of Independence, it was a matter of considerable importance that the only publication on contemporary affairs read by almost all the people from year to year, the book that was a kind of secular Bible, an oracle of knowledge and wisdom to the common people, did, with very few exceptions, enthusiastically support the American cause.

Turning to the New York almanacs, we observe that their share in the evolution of American nationality and independence, like that of the almanacs of the other colonies, involved a double contribution, the dissemination of a common store of facts, ideas, and ideals within and beyond the borders of the province, and the direct cultivation and encouragement of sentiments and trends that assisted in the building of an independent American nation. The very events associated with the printing of the first New York almanac foreshadow several of these forces. The printer William Bradford transferred his printing press from Philadelphia to New York because of active opposition to the governing body of the Quaker city; he was the first man to stand trial in defense of the liberty of the American press; he founded the first newspaper printed in New York; and his business interests, like those of Benjamin Franklin, were intercolonial, his investments being distributed among three colonies, New York, New Jersey, and Pennsylvania. Accordingly, the history of the New York almanacs commenced with a story of revolt against authority and the defense of liberty by a man whose outlook was not provincial. Add to this the fact that the famed Zenger was an apprentice of Bradford, and that printers who later participated in the agitation or rebellion against England had been either his apprentices or apprentices of his apprentices, and you can gauge the significance of this beginning.

The tradition of resistance to tyrannical authority and the guarding of the liberties of the people goes further back, however, than the Bradford trial. We find it flourishing more than forty years before in a remarkable poem printed in the *Danforth* almanac for 1648 celebrating

Figure 3. A Prospective View of part of the Commons (Boston), 1768.

the successful establishment of the Massachusetts Bay colony.[2] The colony is compared to a "thriving plant" at whose roots Astraea, the goddess of justice sits. Each year the young tree

> . . . shoots forth Laws and Libertyes,
> That no mans Will or Wit may tyrannize.
> Those Birds of prey, who sometime have opprest
> And stain'd the Country with their filthy nest
> Justice abhors; & one day hopes to finde
> A way to make all promise-breakers grinde.
> On this tree's top hangs pleasant Liberty,
> Not seen in Austria, France, Spain, Italy.

The poem also tells of the difficulties that attended the planting of the colony and of the rewards that the labor and sacrifices of the founders had secured: not only justice and liberty, but peace, unity, truth, and plenty. It is easy to perceive how much these people cherished the home that they had wrested from the wilderness, a home all the more dear to them because it represented the realization of an ideal, and it is easy to foresee that any attempt to take the control of it away from them would be resisted, if need be, with their lives. These were the seeds which in time blossomed into American patriotism.

A poem of similar significance appeared in the *Titan Leeds* almanac for 1730, entitled, "An Ode to Pennsylvania." Again we are dealing with a colony recently founded by a group of dissenters, who were astonishingly successful in establishing in the American wilderness another commonwealth based on ideal principles. Moreover, it is significant that this poem in praise of Pennsylvania was printed in a New York almanac sold throughout the colonies. Like the poem in the *Danforth* almanac, it reveals a composite of material and spiritual elements, lauding, on the one hand, the wide streets and commercial prosperity of Philadelphia and, on the other, the liberal arts, the peace and liberty, the liberal charter and constitution enjoyed by the colony and its capital. One of the elements in the development of American patriotism among the pioneers of the seventeenth and eighteenth centuries, as among those of the nineteenth, was this feeling of pride in the establishment of a society under the most adverse conditions. This country was literally theirs, hewn out of the hostile wilderness with their own sweat and blood; and it meant more to them than faraway England ever could, even to her native sons.

The New York almanacs, as we have seen, not only reflected the difficulties of the early settlers but also played an important part in overcoming them by advice on many of their problems. We often observe the process of amelioration going on under our very eyes. For instance, the *Daniel Leeds* almanac for 1700 complained of the difficulty of making English wheat grow satisfactorily in this country. At this stage, the settler felt that "this Earth" was "but as a step-mother." In the almanac for 1712 the situation and mood had altered, and we read that "the Colonists already raise more wheat than the West-Indies can take." This transition from hardship to abundance was repeated in countless other phases of life in the new land and was typical of the rapid growth of the colonies during the first century and a half of their existence. The cumulative effect of this growth on the attachment of the colonists to their adopted or native country must have been powerful. In tracing the development of this American consciousness and loyalty, I should mention an interesting piece of evidence left in the New York almanacs. The first New York almanac was entitled: "An Almanack for the Year of Christian Account 1694 . . . . . by Daniel Leeds." The title remained unchanged until 1704, when the word, *American,* was added before *Almanack,* and from that year until 1776 the national designation appeared annually, except in 1729 and 1745, on the title page of one or more New York almanacs.

Throughout the seventeenth century, and well into the eighteenth, there was a constant struggle on the part of the colonies to export enough goods to pay for their imports. The New York almanacs from the beginning were aware of this basic problem and in various ways participated in the efforts of the colonies to become economically independent of England and the other countries from which the imports came. This conflict of economic interest between the mother country and the colonies was an important factor in the evolution of a national sentiment favoring independence.

We find Daniel Leeds declaring as early as 1700:

> This Country exceeds England in affording industrious People the means to be wealthy and flourishing, but a licentious Idleness and Pride obstructs many by pleasurable Horses, fine Houses, gay Household Stuff, shining Garments &c. and though we run in Debt yet these must be had.

If the importation of luxuries was not uncommon in the relatively lean years at the beginning of the century, it grew much worse during the next sixty-odd years. The continuous agitation in the New York almanacs to curtail imports was directed principally against imported alcoholic beverages, tea, and, in the later period, fabrics. Recipes for native substitutes for foreign liquors were eagerly sought and often printed. The *Daniel Leeds* almanac for 1697, for example, announced the result of an experiment to make a stronger drink out of "Syder" and expressed the hope that its general use might help the colonies economically. Apparently, this did not happen, for, fifteen years later, in printing a recipe for "Cider Royal," he warned his readers that the country would remain poor unless they ceased importing foreign liquors. In the almanac of *Titan Leeds* for 1716 they were again reminded to use American grain and fruit for distilling spirits; and the recipes and admonitions continued to appear regularly until the eve of the Revolution.[3]

The introduction of tea early in the century and its rapid advance in popular favor soon attracted the attention of the almanacs. The *Copernicus* almanac for 1747, in its calendar verse for September and October, criticized "modish ladies" for using "Foreign slops," meaning tea and coffee, and urged, since they were harmful to both the physical and economic health of the people:

> Let tid bits then, and triffling tea,
> To toast and buttermilk give way.

The campaign was general. An unnamed writer quoted by Esther Singleton declared in 1734 that

> people that are least able to go to the expence, must have their tea tho' their families want bread. Nay, I am told, often pawn their rings and plate to gratifie themselves in that piece of extravagance.[4]

Tea was a symbol of economic subjection long before the Boston Tea Party.

After about the middle of the century, the stream of propaganda was turned against imported cloth and clothing. *Poor Richard*, 1748, counseled:

> Don't after foreign Food and Clothing roam,
> But learn to eat and wear what's raised at Home.

Hutchins, in the preface to the almanac for 1765, stated that the colonies spent at least £400,000 a year on imported articles and could reduce this amount considerably by economizing on clothing, silks, chinaware, punch, wine, rum, and tea: "And when you must buy Cloaths, let them, I beseech you, be of the Produce of your Country." To give substance to his words, he included an account of the method of "managing wool" used in England:

> Since many of the industrious Farmers of this *and the neighboring Provinces* are now busy in manufacturing Wool, for cloathing their Families and for Use of those Gentlemen who are Well-Wishers of America.

The accompanying list of dutiable articles did not detract from the persuasiveness of the appeal. By this time the movement for economic independence had reached the stage of organization in New York—witness the founding of the "Society for promoting Arts, Agriculture, and Oeconomy in the Province of New York" and the "New York Chamber of Commerce." Of the former a contemporary historian wrote in 1765:

> . . . [It] has a tendency to enrich the inhabitants and make them less dependent on foreign countries for commodities and manufactures.[5]

The almanacs of the other colonies encouraged this policy with equal persistence and fervor. The *Ames* almanac for 1766, for instance, contained such patriotic comments as: "How highly shall we esteem the man that wears the manufactures of his own country, in opposition to the ill taste of the age! Or: "If each blade would mind his trade, each lass and lad in home-spun clad, then we might cramp the growth of stamp." Two years later he wrote more openly:

> Our Fathers came into this Wilderness that they should enjoy their Civil and Religious Liberty. They lived upon boiled Corn and Clams and labored hard to clear and cultivate the Country. Our growing Extravagance have run us amazingly into Debt . . . . [It would help greatly if Americans did not "sip that poisonous Herb, called Bohea Tea" or buy imported woolen goods.] If these wise Measures should be come into, a whole Province will be saved from Slavery and this dreadful Ruin, and we shall soon become a free, rich, and happy people.

The concept of liberty, as set forth in the New York almanacs, was intimately associated with law, property, and the doctrine of "natural rights." The English ideal of a free society stabilized by the legal protection of the person, faith, and property of each individual was even more deeply embedded in the minds of the English settlers in America than in those of their English brothers and was quickly assimilated by the settlers of other nationalities. For example, the first act of the first New York Assembly in 1683 was to frame a charter of liberties which contains the kernel of the Colonial opposition preceding the Revolution. This charter granted freedom of voting to every freeholder and freeman, guaranteed trial by jury, allowed taxation only by consent of the representative Assembly, made martial law illegal, and declared that "no person professing faith in God by Jesus Christ should at any time be in any way disquieted or questioned for any difference of opinion in matters of religion." Although the charter was withdrawn three years later, the ideal embodied in it persisted, and the New York almanacs, being on the popular side, continued to advocate it at every opportunity.

They generally promoted religious toleration according to eighteenth-century standards, holding the view advanced in the *Hutchins* almanac for 1761:

> Persecution for Conscience Sake has occasioned violent Disorders, and vast Effusion of Blood; and to compel Men by Fire and Faggot, to partake even of a delicious Entertainment, is a savage Sort of Hospitality.

In a simple way they occasionally expounded the legal rights of the citizen, as in the *Felix Leeds* almanac for 1727, which includes a short article on the right of appeal for merchants and transient persons from the decisions of the Governor's "Court of Tryals" to the General Assembly, and, in certain cases, to the King's Council. They frequently dwelt on the inequalities and injustices of the legal system arising from inequalities of wealth, and kept alive the feeling of the common man that "the poor and helpless undergo those punishments for small trivial offenses, which the rich and powerful escape for crimes of a much blacker nature."[6] When Hutchins stated in his almanac for 1758 that the billeting of English troops the previous year on the inhabitants of New York City was "against the Constitution, and particularly incompatible with the Declaration of Rights and Privileges of King William and Queen Mary," he was treading on ground long familiar to his readers and was appealing to emotions that were fairly sure to be aroused by that kind of argument.

Another view widely held in the colonies was that general prosperity was impossible without economic liberty, that is, without freedom from restraint in trade and industry, security in the enjoyment of property, and control of taxation. The New York almanacs consistently supported and encouraged this belief. The *Thomas More* almanac for 1753, for example, in discussing the rapid growth of Philadelphia, stated that "liberty" was principally responsible for it. *Roger Sherman* proclaimed in the same year:

> As English Subjects Free-born brave,
> Our Right and Liberties we have,
> Secur'd by good and wholesome Laws,
> Which ought in judging every Cause,
> To be a Standing Rule whereby,
> Each one may have his Property.

The exactions and restraints imposed on the province during the war with France were exceedingly irksome to the people of New York in spite of the fact that they were imposed in time of war. *Roger More,*

1757, for instance, warily printed the address of the inhabitants of Bristol, England, to King George II, in which they demanded an accounting of the immense supplies raised. The following argument must have fallen on very sympathetic ears in this country:

> The Arcana Imperii are well suited to despotick governments, but are inconsistent with and dangerous to the liberties of a free people. Besides, it is no way reconcileable to the nature of our constitution, which is founded on reason and equity, the liberty of the subjects persons, and the security of their properties.

In the next issue, he reverted to the same topic, asserting that liberty was being threatened by the war from without and within and, in conclusion, pleaded for its restoration, predicting that:

> Then, instead of more Trouble, more Losses, and more Taxes, than ever this Land felt before; we should have more Peace, more Plenty, and more Ease than our Enemies wish we should.

The almanac-authors strongly objected to a form of restraint which touched them most closely, the censorship of the press. In the *Roger More* almanac for 1758, the summary of the campaign for the year concluded with an explanation for the reason for not mentioning the defeat of the English at Fort William Henry in the almanac of the previous year. The author stated that the news had been suppressed "by Authority, for what Reason is not for us to say," adding:

> However it may not be amiss here to observe that a Restraint was laid upon the Press and the Year past forbidding any account to be inscribed in the Newspapers of sundry affairs relating to the War, on a Pretence that those Papers were sent as Intelligence to our Enemies at Canada.

This policy, he continued, proved very unwise, for it contributed to the defeat of the English. It would have been much better if Montcalm had known of the great force that was moving against him, since he might not, in that case, have risked a battle. *Hutchins,* in the same year, spoke out more frankly against the government's policy. He maintained that it was "the right of free-born Englishmen, to know and judge for themselves, of the Propriety of Publick Measures," and that the press, "the chief of English Blessings," must always remain "open" in order that "the Commons may not be ignorant of the Transactions on the good or ill Conduct of which their

Liberties, their Properties, and their Lives depend." In Pennsylvania the interference with the freedom of the press occasioned a poetic protest from *Poor Richard* in 1757:

> While free from Force the Press remains,
> *Virtue* and *Freedom* chear our Plains,
> And *Learning* Largesses bestows,
> And keeps unlicens'd open House. . . .
> This *Tree* which Knowledge so affords,
> Inquisitors with flaming Swords
> From Lay-Approach with Zeal defend,
> Lest their own Paradise should end. . . .
> This Nurse of Arts, and Freedom's Fence,
> To chain, is Treason against Sense:
> And *Liberty*, thy thousand Tongues
> None silence who design no Wrongs;
> For those that use the Gag's Restraint,
> First rob, before they stop Complaint.[7]

Soon after the end of the war with France, the Colonial concept of liberty was enlisted again in the sudden conflict with England and served no less effectively as a quickening and unifying slogan. The *Freeman* almanac, an organ of the Sons of Liberty, which first appeared in 1767, broadcast it in every issue:

> Oh Liberty Heaven's choice Prerogative!
> True bond of Law, thou social Soul of Property,
> Thou Breath of Reason, Life of Life, itself![8]

The *Roger More* almanac for 1770 entitled a poem on the benefits of liberty: "The Genius of America to her Sons." Another poem in the same almanac, "On Publick Liberty,"[9] illustrated the ideas and emotions that were being spurred by the New York almanacs at the time—democracy, resistance to tyranny, and the doctrine of natural, consitutional, and charter rights and privileges. The noble and unselfish political leadership, Roger More continued, which had once wedded right to might and established the liberty and security of the people, had since degenerated into corrupt tyrannical government:

> Hence all the evils which mankind have known,
> The priest's dark mystery, the tyrant's throne;
> Hence Lords and Ministers; and such sad things,
> And hence the strange divinity of kings.

Englishmen, however, were not men to submit to exploitation:

Curse on all laws, which liberty subdue,
And make the many wretched for the few . . .
But thou, great Liberty, keep Britain free,
Nor let men use us as we use the bee.
Let not base drones upon our honey thrive,
And suffocate the maker in his hive.

The almanacs of the other colonies expressed essentially the same
point of view.

The New York almanacs also exemplified and fostered a colonial
trait that appeared early and contributed to the ultimate independence
and union of the colonies—a critical attitude toward custom, tradition,
and authority. The special conditions arising from the settlement of
the American wilderness were primarily responsible for the development of this American trait, but the almanacs helped it along. The absence of censorship allowed the almanac-authors to speak freely in
times of peace and war and to apply the Colonial independence of
thought to every important phase of contemporary life, particularly
science, religion, and politics. In the New York almanacs, all of which
were printed after the Revolution of 1688 had established a limited
monarchy, the attitude toward the king or queen as the symbol of
tradition and authority, was generally respectful but never uncritical.
Each received the due allotment of pious wishes, but was not permitted to forget that "Scepters are as brittle as Reeds."[10]

A poem on custom in the *Titan Leeds* almanac for 1738 illustrates
this independence very clearly. A thing was not right, the poem observed, just because it was old. While custom should guide men, it
should never blind them. The king, for instance, thought that the
"Homage Fools have paid, becomes his Due." Yet, the very fact that
he appealed to tradition was a confession of his weakness, proving
that he did not rule by divine right. Again, in religion, custom had
confused human and divine doctrines and passed the mixed product
on from age to age. In truth, we owed reverence to our forebears, but
not to their crimes and follies.

When the Laws of Nature are so plain,
Custom's impertinent, Tradition's vain.

When the conflict with England reached a climax, the leaders of the
rebellion could appeal to a people long freed from the habit of blind
obedience to tradition and authority, a habit which the almanacs
printed in New York and the other colonies had helped to break.

As we have often observed, the war with France came at a turning
point in the growth of the colonies and hastened and accentuated
many tendencies. Among those were the forces which were slowly

pushing the colonists toward national independence. The New York almanacs, which had been enlarged to make room for the additional patriotic appeals and the annual summaries of the campaigns, were an important link in the diffusion of these forces by the almanacs. The prefaces expanded into editorials of exhortation or criticism; the calendar verses duplicated the material of the prefaces and summaries in metrical form; and the rest of the contents were adapted to the needs and demands of the war. When the war was over, the problems inherited from it took up the slack, and a further enlargement was necessary. It was in these two critical decades before the Revolution that the educative function of the Colonial almanac was most consistently and usefully pursued, attaining the peak of its influence.

The habit of the New York almanac-authors of examining facts, and events objectively and without regard to tradition or authority was at once transferred to the British conduct of the war. They were prompt to acknowledge merit, but equally ready to expose inefficiency and error. British defeats were analyzed and their military and naval plans criticized without hesitation. For example, Roger More[11] took Braddock to task for waiting from March to July in 1755 before starting out for Fort Duquesne; Shirley, for not attacking Niagara, according to the plan, before September of the same year, when it was too late; and Johnson, for not following up the victory over the French at Fort George. He declared that if the British had attacked in the spring, when the St. Lawrence and Ohio rivers were hardly ever navigable, the French would have been caught unprepared and would surely have been defeated. The conduct of these campaigns was so flagrantly inept that they constituted in his opinion sufficient ground for a legislative investigation. As a result of these open criticisms, the respect of the colonists for the British army was seriously undermined, while the American successes in the field were widely heralded in the almanacs, creating a general feeling of confidence in American military ability which was not diminished by the reports of Americans who had fought side by side with the British and felt that they were their equals, if not their superiors, as soldiers. The significance of this widespread belief cannot be overestimated as a factor in the ultimate decision of the colonists to risk armed rebellion against England. There is dramatic prophecy in the first appearance during these war years of names which were to occupy a prominent place on the scroll of Revolutionary heroes—Isaac Sears and Alexander McDougall as commanders of privateers from New York,[12] and George Washington as the leader of a mission from the government of Virginia to negotiate with the French regarding their encroachments on the Ohio and as the commander of the expedition that fortified Fort Duquesne and was defeated there by the French in 1754.[13]

The colonists were also getting a lesson on the prizes for which nations fight and the material rewards that attend victory. For instance, the *Hutchins* almanac for 1759, after telling its readers about the great victories at Cape Breton and Frontenac, remarked that the English, at the expense of only 172 men killed and about 350 wounded, had gained possession of an island on which the French in the year before the war had cured fish and derived blubber-oil worth 949,192 pounds. The impression left by information of this kind could be easily transferred to the prospects of economic benefits to be derived from independence.

The New York almanacs also bore witness to the ironic fact that the war brought about a closer cultural rapprochement between France and the colonies. The newspapers printed numerous advertisements of French teachers, and a greater number of French books, including the works of Rabelais, Racine, Voltaire, Montesquieu, and Rousseau, were placed on sale by booksellers in both the North and the South.[14] Voltaire was first introduced to New York almanac readers in 1758 by *Roger More* through extracts from his satirical romance, *Scarmentado*, which *More* affirmed contained "more good Advice than the whole Almanack is worth." The previously mentioned essay on education in his almanac for 1761[15] shows the influence of Rousseau. The liberal social theories popularized by *Freeman, Hutchins, Roger More*, and other almanac-authors during the pre-Revolutionary decade probably owed much to French thinkers.

Perhaps the most important result of the war was the impetus it gave to the idea of a union of all the colonies. The advisability of it was apparent, but England, for reasons of her own, was reluctant to encourage it. The early reverses of the British forces, however, alarmed the colonies and hurried them into combining their resources and working out a unified strategy. The almanacs quickly fell in with the idea. *Hutchins,* for example, in his almanac for 1758 earnestly pleaded for the adoption of this policy, asserting that

> . . . our Militia well-disciplined, and properly commanded, will when ever we pay a due Regard, and form a rational Plan for our Preservation, by a vigorous Exertion of the united Force of our Colonies redeem our Country from the Evils we feel, and prevent the impending Ruin which must otherwise infallibly ensue.

The success which followed their united efforts made them fully aware for the first time of their potential strength in confederation, a fact which they never forgot during the conflict that commenced soon after the end of the war. When the need for effective protest arose, the advantages of concerted action had already been demonstrated, and the method of organization was familiar. How thoroughly the experience in cooperation had been assimilated may be illustrated by the following extract from an article on public liberty printed in *Philo's*

Essex Almanack (Salem, Massachusetts) for 1770:

> Let these Truths be indelibly impressed on our Minds—
> that we cannot be happy without being free—that we
> cannot be free without being secure in our Property—
> that we cannot be secure in our Property, if without our
> Consent, others may, as by Right, take it away—that
> Taxes imposed on us by Parliament do thus take it
> away—that Duties laid for the sold Purposes of raising
> Money, are Taxes—that Attempts to lay such Duties
> should be firmly opposed—and that this Opposition can
> never be effectual, unless it is by our united Efforts. [16]

With the French danger removed, another strand in the weakening bond between the colonies and the mother country snapped. This
eventuality, which had been foreseen by both the colonists and the
English for some time, had acted as a brake on the desire of England
to destroy French power in North America. There was a hint of the
dilemma which the British Government faced in the preface to the
Thomas More almanac for 1749. Congratulating the reader on the prospect of a year of peace, the author added:

> Our Brethren on the Frontiers may now follow their law-
> ful Occupations, without any Fear of having their Scalps
> carried away by a barbarous Enemy; and none of them
> be tempted to go abroad on Expeditions which was
> never design'd to be put in Execution, Such Things, My
> Friends, lead me to think our Mother Country, like a
> kind and tender Parent who thinks her Children have
> grown too high-minded for their good, has contrived
> great part of these Measures, in order to correct and
> humble us a little, lest we should live too well, and kick
> at her.

The Swedish botanist Peter Kalm, who traveled in England and
the colonies from 1748 to 1751, wrote:

> I have been told by Englishmen, and not only by such as
> were born in America, but even by such as came from
> Europe, that the English colonies in North-America, in
> the space of thirty or fifty years, would be able to form a
> state by themselves, entirely independent on Old En-
> gland. But, as the whole country which lies along the sea
> shore, is unguarded, and on the land side is harassed by
> the French, in times of war these dangerous neighbours
> are sufficient to prevent the connection of the colonies

with their mother country from being quite broken off. The English government has therefore sufficient reason to consider the French in North-America, as the best means of keeping the colonies in their due submission.[17]

The knowledge of the rapid growth of the colonies in population intensified the consciousness of strength which the war had made evident. The population statistics frequently printed in the almanacs during the century kept the people well informed in this respect.[18] At the time of the war with France, they numbered well over a million, while the French in America totalled only 52,000.[19] The morale of the reader could not but be reinforced by this comparison. *Rivington's* almanac for 1775 predicted that North America would contain 20 million inhabitants in 1830.[20] The prospect was dazzling: "If we may judge by Analogy," exclaimed *Thomas More* in 1765, "and the progressive Increase of the Inhabitants of this Continent, the Kingdoms of the Earth and the Glory of the World will be translated into America."

It is hardly any wonder that the more enterprising and imaginative of the colonists were determined at any cost to retain control of a country whose destiny promised to be so glorious. *Nathaniel Ames* was, therefore, voicing the thoughts and hopes of a voiceless multitude when, in his almanac for 1758, he penned this splendidly prophetic vision of the America of the future:

> Arts and Sciences will change the Face of Nature in their Tour from Hence over the Appalachian Mountains to the Western Ocean; and as they march thro' the vast Desert, the Residence of Wild Beasts will be broken up, and their obscene Howl cease for ever—Instead of which the Stones and Trees will dance together at the Music of Orpheus—the Rocks will disclose their hidden Gems— and the inestimable Treasures of Gold & Silver be broken up. Huge Mountains of Iron Ore are already discovered; and vast Stores are reserved for future Generations. This Metal more useful than Gold and Silver, will imploy Millions of Hands, not only to form the martial Sword, and peaceful Share, alternately; but an Infinity of Utensils improved in the Exercise of Art, and Handicraft amongst Men . . . . Shall not then those vast Quarries, that teem with mechanic Stone—those for Structure be piled into great Cities—and those for Sculpture into Statues to perpetuate the Honor of renowned Heroes . . . O! Ye unborn Inhabitants of America! Should this Page escape its destin'd Conflagration at the Year's End, and these Alphabetical Letters remain

> legible—when your Eyes behold the Sun after he has rol-
> led the Seasons round for two or three Centuries more,
> you will know that in Anno Domini 1758, we dream'd of
> your Times.[21]

One of the leading factors in the swift increase of population was,
of course, the relatively great tide of immigration that flowed into the
colonies during the first half of the century. Most of these immigrants
were German or Scotch-Irish—a fact which affected the intensity and
magnitude of the rebellion against England, since the Germans were
not bound to her by ties of national sentiment and the Scotch-Irish felt
only hatred for her.

The additional burden of immigration added to the difficulties of
economic readjustment after the war with France, and these, in turn,
constituted an important aggravating element in the temper of the
colonists during the dispute with England. The New York and other
almanacs testify again and again to the "hard times" that followed the
war. The *New York Pocket Almanack* and the *Thomas More* almanac for
1764, in printing an abstract of a recent law designed to check the rise
in prices, spoke of the ruinous effect on the lower classes; and the
Hutchins and *Thomas More* almanacs for 1768 still lamented the bad
times and scarcity of money. Nathaniel Ames remarked in his almanac for 1766:

> I should conclude, did I not share in the general distress
> of my countrymen, and think it out of character, not to
> condole with them in their present distressed cir-
> cumstances, who not only groan, but almost sink be-
> neath a load of debt; our merchants continually breaking;
> no money to be had, even for the most valuable articles;
> and all threatened with ruin, without the lenity and as-
> sistance of our superiors; yet so far from this, that we are
> shocked with a new demand, which it is thought by
> many all the current specie among us is not able to
> satisfy; and after that is gone, then go houses and lands,
> then liberties![22]

England could not have chosen a more inopportune time to mod-
ify her general policy toward the colonies. The urgent appeals to the
colonists to resist the French attempt to encroach on their liberties and
possessions were still fresh in their minds; and the war had taught
them that their united strength was great and that the English war
machine was vulnerable.

The first stage of the clash, as it was represented in the New
York almanacs, started with the agitation over the Stamp Act. The
reaction of the almanac-authors ranged from sullen acquiescence to

dignified protest. Thomas More declared:

> Those who do not purchase this Almanack now must
> pay smartly for it after the first Day of November next—
> It is a Tax we must pay; and what we cannot help, let us
> endure with Patience; that being the only comfort we
> have, if any comfort at all is likely to come from its Es-
> tablishment. [23]

Hutchins was more frank,[24] stating that the tax was "by no means
agreeable to the Publick, and very disagreeable to the Printer," since
it increased the price of a dozen almanacs by four shillings and
threatened to reduce the sale of almanacs considerably. The tax thus
antagonized a class whose assistance was indispensable if the colonists were to organize a united protest against the measure. In 1766
Roger More, in a remarkably farsighted preface, set forth practically
the entire line of reasoning by which the colonists were to justify resistance to English authority during the next decade. He began
solemnly:

> The Design of my former Prefaces was, to amuse, or
> make you smile; but now, when we see a dreadful Storm
> of Ruin just bursting over our Heads, and hear its Thun-
> ders roar, such Lightness would be neither proper nor
> excusable.

If the attack on the liberty of the colonies, he continued, had been
made by a professed foe, it would have been less shocking, but who
would have ever suspected it of England,

> whose Glory it is above all the People upon the Face of
> the Earth, to be the guardians of Liberty, and Defenders
> of the Rights of the Oppressed in every Quarter of the
> Globe?

This affliction must have been visited upon them as a punishment for
their wickedness.

> Let us then repent . . . and earnestly implore Forgive-
> ness and Protection of God, and he will have Mercy
> upon us and save us.

In the meantime, however,

> let us with Firmness and invincible Resolution, tho' with
> becoming Decency and Respect, assert our Rights, and

use every prudent Measure for their Preservation. Let us find Means to convey our Complaints to the European Sovereign . . . . Let Him, and each Body of the Legislature, and every Man of Power and Influence in England, be for ever wearied with out Complaints and Remonstrances and Petitions . . . let them be incessant and perpetual, from General to Generation . . . till we obtain Redress . . . . If Death should be the consequence of this honest Plainness, which is our indispensible Duty, let us disdain a Thought of Fear . . . How glorious would it be to die in such a Cause!

In conclusion, he set forth the reasons for the protest:

The very Life and Soul and Spirit of the English Laws and Constitution is that we shall be bound by no Laws but of our own making, nor taxed but by our own Consent, given by Representatives of our own Choosing . . . . Nor tried, but by our own Peers . . . . These Rights are founded in the Law of Nature, which is the Law of God, eternal and immutable.

Then, quoting chapter and verse, he suggested:

Our Constitutional Laws declare, that Acts of Parliament that are against common Justice and Reason, or are impossible to be perform'd, should be judged void, . . . and the whole Spirit and Soul of the English Law is to the same Effect.

The main lines of defense were thus drawn by this New York almanac at the very outset of the conflict. The English Constitution and the Natural Rights of Man would be the principal bulwarks in argument, and the campaign for the protection of Colonial interests would be respectful, but unyielding and continuous.

The repeal of the Stamp Act was hailed in the almanacs for the following year with unbounded enthusiasm and rejoicing; Pitt and the King were gratefully lauded; and all looked forward to peace and prosperity. The *Roger More* almanac for 1768 inaugurated the second stage of the struggle, during which it became apparent that England did not intend to yield to the Colonial point of view, and the colonies would try to arrive at a peaceful solution without retreating from their position. This issue reported to its readers that they must not fall into a state of deluded optimism. Times were still bad; the battle for the defense of their rights and liberties was not yet over; and they must remain united and ever vigilant. In the next almanac he urged them to remain firm in their patriotism, even at the price of death, and to refuse to submit to "Ministerial Pride and Avarice."

At this stage, the New York almanacs were engaged, on the one hand, in sustaining the morale of the rebellious colonists and, on the other, in hinting at what would happen if England persisted in her repressive policy. The colonists were constantly reminded in prose and verse of the sacred duty of defending their liberty and property. Those who set personal gain above their country's welfare were roundly cursed.[25] Many of the proverbs and stories reflected the contemporary agitation indirectly, employing such themes as the fragility of arbitrary power, the ideal type of king, the danger of indifference to the general welfare, and the doctrine of equality. A few instances drawn from the proverbs follow:

Arbitrary power is like most other things that are very hard, they are also very apt to break.[26]

Happy that King who is great by justice, and that people who are free by obedience.[27]

The sole end of government is the happiness of the people.[28]

He that boasts his Ancestors, confesseth he has no Virtue of his own.[29]

What difference is there betwixt a Prince and a peasant? No more than between two bricks all made of the same clay; only one is placed on the top of a turret, and the other in the bottom of a well.[30]

The colonists ostentatiously affirmed their loyalty to England and the King, but usually appended the qualification that, as true Englishmen, they would defend their rights and liberties with their lives. Ominous signs of the seriousness of this intention were not lacking. A metrical "Address to Britannia" printed in the *Roger More* almanac for 1771 warned England that the peril to her safety and prosperity from "perfidious Gaul, or haughty Spain" was slight compared to that created by "slaves in office" who disregarded the protests of the oppressed and the rights of freemen. The fate of kings who condoned misrule was frequently alluded to with obvious reference to contemporary conditions; witness these last lines from a modernized version of one of Gower's tales included in the *Hutchins* almanac for 1769:

> . . . If the common people cry,
> And their proud monarch ask not why;
> Or told, refuses to redress,

And make unnumber'd burdens less;
Or careless seeks in sports and play,
To pass the jocund hours away;
Tho' hunger, penury, and toil
Afflict his Subjects all the while;
Their fate, at length, becomes his own.

In the meantime, the almanac-authors in New York and the other colonies were of great assistance to the leaders of the party which faced the prospect of going beyond words in the event that the British government refused to retreat from its position. Nine years before Concord and Lexington, the *Roger More* and *Hutchins* almanacs quietly printed information that revealed the determination of this party to risk armed resistance, if necessary. Both of these almanacs contained instructions on how to cast shot from lead and how to "use an Horse to Fire-arms," and the *Hutchins* added an article describing the method of preparing potash from oak wood followed in Hungary, Poland, and Germany. The *Freeman* almanac for 1769 told its readers how to make gunpowder. In the third and last stage of the pre-Revolutionary conflict, the purpose of these inclusions was openly avowed. The *Hutchins* almanac for 1776 printed a summary of Benjamin Rush's account of the manufacture of saltpeter with the explanation that the "making of Salt-Petre is now become an Object of such Consequence to the Publick," and the *Ames* almanac for 1775 coupled a receipt for making gunpowder with verses urging Americans to unite and take up arms, and assuring them that, while they wore no dazzling armor, they could shoot as "sure as death." The service which the almanacs thus rendered to the Revolutionary cause was of inestimable value. It was fortunate for the colonists that it probably never occurred to the British authorities to sample the common almanacs.

The almanacs for 1775 and 1776 informed their readers of the extent to which the resistance of the colonies had been organized and of the imminence of armed revolt. The *Gaine's Register* for 1775 contained the provisions and recommendations of the "Association of the Continental Congress" of 1774, the conclusion of which was a virtual declaration of independence and sovereignty:

All and each of which the aforesaid deputies in behalf of themselves, and their constituents, do claim, demand, and insist on, as their indubitable rights and liberties; which cannot be legally taken from them, altered or abridged by any power whatever, without their own consent, by their representatives in their several provincial legislatures.

The logical consequence of this declaration appeared in *Gaine's New York Pocket Almanack* for 1776, in which was listed for the first time the "Staff of the Army of the Thirteen United Provinces in N. America, as accurately as could be obtained Oct. 10, 1775."

As the time of the outbreak of hostilities approached, the New York almanacs cooperated, as we should anticipate, in marshalling their readers for the revolutionary step. The *Father Hutchins* almanac for 1776, for example, attempted to prove the lawfulness of war by biblical examples and even utilized the mating instinct as illustrated by the poem, "The Stipulation":

> A While, Fond Damon, prithee tarry,
> Nor woo me, to thy eager arms:
> Oh! Thinkst thou this a time to marry,
> When all our country's in alarms?
> In holy wedlock shall we join,
> Our land when wild invasion braves?
> Or would'st thou wish to have me thine,
> To propagate a brood of slaves?
> Now Furbish up thy armour bright,
> And first thy valour let me see!
> Who for his country fears to fight,
> I fear will never stand by me.
> Then buckle on thy trusty sword,
> And when our vanquish'd foes are fled,
> I promise, then, upon my word,
> To take thee to my virgin bed.

The MS notes found in several copies of the New York almanacs of this period, many of them by John Moore, a minor loyalist official in the government of New York, afford contemporary evidence of the conflict. The copy of *Gaine's Universal Register* for 1775 in the Library of Congress describes the organized methods employed by the rebel party to prevent the unloading of goods from British ships and the incident of the removal of the cannon from the Battery by the same party. The copy of *Gaine's New York Pocket Almanack* for 1776 in the New York Historical Society contains interesting loyalist comments on the Declaration of Independence and the Battle of White Plains:

> this fatal day Independy declared by the Congress— Rivers of Blood will flow in consequence of it—no Peace for many Years.

> Battle at White Plains. Rebels defeated but not pursued—Genl. Howe says, the River Bronx prevented

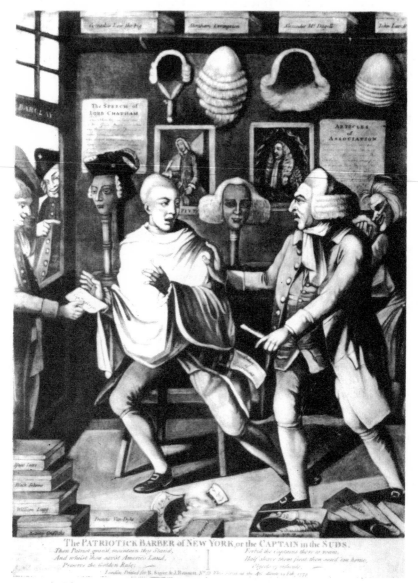

Figure 4. "The Patriotick Barber of New York, or the Captain in the Suds," 1774.

it—NB a Boy can jump over it & Plenty of wood for Bridges if necessary. Loyalists convinced Genl. Howe does not do his duty nor mean to conquer the Country.

In *Gaine's* register for 1781 on the interleaved page after the October calendar, we read:

Lord Cornwallis capitulated. I presume this is the finishing Stroke to the War and that Am. Independence is established.[31]

Finally, the entry against March 17 in *Gaine's* pocket almanac for 1783 marks the unhappy ending of the loyalist cause:

Packet Capt. Bolders arrived with 3 Mails & Articles between Britain & America. N.B. much such a conclusion, I had long ago expected great distress will be experienced by many many thousd. faithful Subjects, and I suspect no good eventually to this my native country please God I will remain, Whig & Rebel violence notwithstanding.[32]

In the difficult decade after the Revolution, the New York almanacs, besides continuing as before to keep their readers informed on the important events of the year, were occupied principally in resisting the forces of reaction and disintegration which generally follow in the train of revolution. They quickly adapted themselves to the changed order and helped thereby to establish continuity between the past and present and to give form and stability to the new nation, which was still uncertain and disordered. The old almanac looked comfortably the same. If the word *Columbian* displaced the word *British* on the title page, or revolutionary anniversaries were added on the calendar page, the alteration was made unobtrusively and was far outweighed by the absence of change in the general appearance, arrangement, and contents of the almanac. The Man of Signs still squatted familiarly in his accustomed place; the weather predictions were as vague as ever; and the anniversary of the martyrdom of King Charles I and the birthday of George III cohabited peacefully with the anniversary of the Declaration of Independence and the birthday of George Washington.

We leave the almanacs at this turning point in the history of the American people. They had assisted inconspicuously in the building of an American nation on this continent, helping the colonists to overcome the hardships and handicaps of life in the wilderness, carrying a common cultural inheritance among the scattered and isolated communities along the Atlantic seaboard, and bringing in tabloid form to the most remote settlements the important activities, accomplishments, and happenings of the age. They lent encouragement to the qualities of tolerance and self-reliance naturally bred by the conditions of the frontier, supported the trend of the colonies toward independence, aided in the development of an American consciousness, and, in the fateful years preceding the Revolution, helped to organize the united resistance of the colonies and to make accessible to all the people the principles and ideals for which they finally risked their lives and possessions.

Retrospective

The remarkably varied contents of the New York and other Colonial almanacs of the eighteenth century indicate that these popular little periodicals were an integral part of the life and thought of America during that century. In a limited way, they reflected the predominant interests and activities of the age and presented the principal economic, political, and cultural developments of the century in a simplified and abbreviated form adapted to the needs and preferences of their readers. Through these annual periodicals, the common people of America were able to keep in contact with contemporary trends and events during a period when the geographic and economic handicaps of Colonial life put books, magazines, or newspapers beyond the reach of most of them. The study of the Colonial almanac of the eighteenth century, therefore, has a twofold value: It helps us to rediscover to some extent what the common people of the colonies thought and believed and how they lived, and it reveals how much the almanac contributed to the building of the American nation and character.

The New York almanacs indicate that their readers were interested mainly in history, science, and government. Theology, after the first quarter of the century, was relegated to a secondary position, but the result of the impact of sciencific method and discovery on the fundamental tenets and practices of the Christian religion continued to interest the readers. A more tolerant attitude toward differences of creed among Protestants, a greater emphasis on ethics as the essence of true religion, and a less anthropomorphic conception of God are discernible. A more sympathetic attitude toward the Indians apparently attended this rationalistic tendency. It was recognized that the Indian side of the story of European conquest and colonization was not quite flattering to the supposedly superior race and that Christian deeds often had not agreed with Christian teachings. In the latter part of the century the Indian was regarded by many as the embodiment of Rousseau's sentimental ideal of the "noble savage." Intermarriage between the two races was evidently not very strongly disapproved.

Historical information was imparted by the almanacs chiefly

through curious facts and incidents, dramatic episodes, and chronologies, that is, dated lists of important events, usually drawn from American history, and stressing economic, social, and cultural history. The scientific instruction, except that in astronomy and physics, was of a practical kind intended mainly for use on the farm—agricultural advice, household hints, and simple medical and hygienic information. Many of the medical items, however, were obviously intended for the use of physicians of very limited training, a class which constituted a majority of the profession.

It would appear from the evidence of the almanacs that the average colonist enjoyed few comforts and conveniences before the fourth decade of the century. Many of them, in fact, were living at the beginning of the century in a state scarcely above the primitive level of the surrounding Indians. Food, however, was comparatively plentiful, land was cheap, and early and prolific marriages were prevalent. After the fourth decade, the improvement of material conditions was rapid and was greatly stimulated by the war with France. The almanacs shared in the prosperity of this period. During the preceding period, William Bradford had practically monopolized the printing business of New York, and the *Leeds* almanac printed by him had dominated the New York field. In the next period, however, many new printers and almanacs competed for the increased business, the most successful being the printers James Parker and Hugh Gaine, and the *More* and *Hutchins* almanacs printed by them respectively. Sheet almanacs, Dutch almanacs, pocket almanacs, and, finally, almanac-registers were developed to meet the greater demand. Since the competition was intense and copyright laws were still unknown, the "pirating" of successful issues flourished, giving rise to acrimonious disputes between printers expressed in coarse, abusive language.

The literary significance of the almanac is to be measured not by the fact that most of the verse and prose selections are mediocre in quality and imitative in type and style, but rather by a comparison of the probable literary knowledge and appreciation of the common people of America at the beginning of the century with the average literary level of the almanacs. From that point of view, we must grant that the almanacs raised the literary standards of the American people, introduced them to many of the great authors of English and world literature, and provided them with literary models appropriate to their stage of education at that time. It is also less important that the almanacs contained little original verse and prose of permanent literary value than that they offered the amateur writers among the colonists an opportunity, however limited, to publish their original literary compositions.

Finally it should not be overlooked that many of the selections were of excellent quality. This is true not only of the selections of such writers as Shakespeare, Milton, Bacon, Dryden, Pope, Swift, the

Appendix A

Reference List of New York City Almanacs (1694–1793)

Daniel Leeds, 1694–1713
Titan Leeds, 1714–1744*
Felix Leeds, 1727, 1728, 1730
John Clapp, 1697, 1699
Daniel Travis, 1709–1719
B. A. Philo-Astro, 1723
William Birkett, 1728–1743
John Hughes, 1726, 1728
Copernicus, 1745–1747
J. Gale, 1748–1751
Roger Sherman, 1750–54
W. Jones, 1750
Thomas More, 1746–1755, 1760–1768
Roger More, 1756–1773
John N. Hutchins, 1747–1793
G. Christopher, 1754–1755
Jesse Parsons, 1757
Father Abraham, 1759
Freeman, 1767–72

Mark Time, 1774
Wing Reviv'd, 1762–1764**
Merry Andrew, 1774–1775
Richard Meanwell, 1774–1775
J. Rivington, 1774–1775
New-York and Country, 1776
Father Hutchins, 1776
Bickerstaff, 1778–1779
U. S. Almanack, 1782, 1786, 1787, 1789
Stearns Universal Kalendar 1783–1784
C. Webster, 1784
Town & Country, 1784
Poor Will Improved, 1785–1786
Loudon, 1785–1787
Columbian Almananack, 1788–1792
Greenleaf, 1791–1793
Father Hutchins Revived 1790–1793

*Not printed in 1727; title for 1744: *Dead Man's Almanack.*
**Title for 1764: *Wing Improv'd.*

143

Appendix B

Summary of Contents of
Freeman's New-York Almanack, for 1768

Title page
>Summary of contents
>Verses on the limitation of human knowledge

Preface by Frank Freeman

Letter to Mr. Freeman by "Fatidicus"
>An obviously fictitious letter satirizing astrology

Verses on man's inability to foresee the future

Paragraph, "The Power of Gold"

Poem, "The Lottery Ticket"

"The Rose: a Fable" (in verse)

Verses on the golden mean

"Eclipses in 1768"

"Names and Characters of the Seven Planets, so called"

"The Five Aspects."

"The Twelve Signs, with the Parts of the Body they are supposed to govern"

"Explanation" on the use of the calendar

"Vulgar Notes for 1768"

"An Ephemeris of the Planet's Motions for the 1st, 6th, 11th, 16th, 21st, and 26th Day of each Month, 1768"

Calendar for January
>First eight lines of poem on humanity
>"Observable Days"
>Weather predictions
>Signs of the moon for each day
>Time of rising and setting of sun for each day
>The hour nearest to the moon's rising and setting for each day
>The hour nearest to the moon's southing
>The hour nearest to "High-Water, at New York, Elizabeth-Town Point", New London, and "Tarpaulin-Cove"
>The day of the "Moon's Age"

Proverbs:
"Think of three Things, whence you came, where you are going, and to whom you must Account."
"Business is the Salt of Life."
Page opposite January calendar
Poem, "New-Year"
Poem, "Winter"
"How to save Charges in Fuel"
February calendar page
Page opposite February calendar
Beginning of essay on law and lawyers by "Probus"
March calendar page
Page opposite March calendar
Continuation of essay on law and lawyers
April calendar page
Page opposite April calendar
Conclusion of essay on law and lawyers
May calendar page
Page opposite May calendar
Poem, "A Fable for those that go to Law"
"Thoughts upon several Subjects" e.g. "All honest Men should enter into an Association to support one another against the common Enemy, without having any other Interest at Heart but that of the public Good, or being influenced by any other Passion than the Love of their Country."
June calendar page
Page opposite June calendar
Continuation of "Thoughts upon several Subjects"
July calendar page
Page opposite July calendar
Continuation of "Thoughts upon several Subjects"
August calendar page
Page opposite August calendar
Continuation of "Thoughts upon several Subjects"
September calendar page
Page opposite September calendar
Conclusion of "Thoughts upon several Subjects"
Poem, "The Old Bachelor's Lamentation"
October calendar page
Page opposite October calendar
Conclusion of poem, "The Old Bachelor's Lamentation"
Poem, "On a Watch-Case"
Poem, "On a Horse-Racer"
November calendar page
Page opposite November calendar
Poem, "The properest Day to Drink"

Poem, "On Wit and Raillery"
Poem, "The Loyal Pair"
Poem, "For a Watch"
December calendar page
Page opposite December calendar
    Announcement regarding courts
    Time and place of meeting of Supreme Courts of New Jersey
    Verses on the planet Venus
    Correction of errors on following pages
Time and place of Quaker General Meetings
Information about "Stage Waggons from Powles's Hook Ferry"
Rates, etc. of "other Stages from New-York to Philadelphia"
Time and place of meeting of Supreme Courts, Courts of Sessions
    and Common Pleas, of New York
Time and place of meeting of Supreme Courts, Courts of Quarter Ses-
    sions, County Courts for Pleas, of New Jersey
Time and place of meeting of Superior and Inferior Courts of Connec-
    ticut
Time and place of meeting of Superior and Inferior Courts of Rhode
    Island
Receipts.
    Ten pages of receipts
Table of Interest at 7 per Cent
Verses on importance of having money.
"A tide-Table"
Verses on inconstancy of human life
"Ages and Names of all the Monarchs in Europe"
"A Table of the Value and Weight of Coins, as they now pass in En-
    gland, New-York, Connecticut, Philadelphia, and Quebec
Verses on liberty
"A List of his Majesty's Council for the Province of New-York"
"Officers in Chancery"
"Officers in the Supreme Court of Judicature"
"Public Notaries"
"List of the General Assembly for the Province of New-York"
"Officers in the Court of Admiralty"
"Civil Officers in the City of New-York"
"Vestrymen"
"Custom-House Officers"
"A List of his Majesty's Council for the Province of New-Jersey"
"List of the General Assembly"
Roads and postage rates
    From New York to Charleston
    From Philadelphia to Pittsburg and Bethlehem
    From Philadelphia to Lancashire
    From New York to Quebec

From Rutland, Vermont, to Albany
From Boston to Plymouth and Cape Cod
Circuit road on Long Island
"Distance to Missisippi"
Postage rates and regulations established by Act of Parliament, October 10, 1765
Poem on betrayers of their country

Appendix C

Reference List of Selected Almanacs of Other Colonies

Nathaniel Ames (Boston), 1731, 1733, 1734, 1750–1752, 1766, 1773, 1775
Anderson improved (Newport, Rhode Island), 1775
Atkin's *Kalendarium Pennsilvaniense,* 1685
Danforth Almanack (Cambridge, Massachusetts), 1646, 1648
Foster's Almanack (Cambridge, Massachusetts), 1675
Freebetter's Connecticut Almanack, 1774
John Jerman (Philadelphia), 1731
Daniel Leeds ("near Philadelphia"), 1687
Nathaniel Low (Boston), 1768
Cotton Mather's *Boston Ephemeris,* 1683
Nathanael Mather's *Boston Ephemeris,* 1685
The New-England Diary, Or, Almanack (Boston), 1723
New-Jersey, Pennsylvania, Delaware, Maryland and Virginia Almanac (Baltimore, Maryland), 1791
Osborne's (Portsmouth, New Hampshire), 1787
Poor Richard (Philadelphia), 1733–1758, 1763, 1787
Poor Robin (Newport, Rhode Island), 1728
South-Carolina Almanack (Charlestown), 1760
Stafford's Almanac (New Haven, Connecticut), 1778
Stearns Universal Calendar (Bennington, Vermont), 1790
John Tobler's *Pennsylvania . . . Almanack* (Wilmington, Delaware), 1773
John Tobler's *South-Carolina & Georgia Almanack* (Charlestown, S. C.), 1767
Timothy Trueman (Trenton, New Jersey), 1781
John Tulley (Boston), 1687
The Virginia Almanack (Williamsburg), 1753
Theophilus Wreg's *Virginia Almanack* (Williamsburg), 1762
Robert Andrews's *Virginia Almanack* (Richmond), 1792
Whittemore's Almanack (Boston), 1719

Notes and References

Chapter One

I am greatly indebted in this chapter to Isaiah Thomas's *History of Printing in America* and Charles Hildeburn's *Sketches of Printers and Printing in Colonial New York*. See Selected Bibliography.

1. Charles F. Horne, *History of the State of New York* (Boston: D. C. Heath & Co., 1916), pp. 27ff.

2. Robert Rogers, *A Concise Account of North America* (London, 1765), p. 65.

3. William Bradford, John Peter Zenger, Hugh Gaine, and James Rivington were born in Europe; James Parker was born in Woodbridge, New Jersey, William Weyman in Pennsylvania, and John Holt in Virginia.

4. The first almanac printed by William Bradford and the first almanac printed in Pennsylvania was Samuel Atkins's *Kalendarium Pennsilvaniense* for 1686.

5. Isaiah Thomas and others were mistaken about the day of his birth, which they give as the 20th or 29th. The May 20th date was quoted from *Titan Leeds, 1739*. But, on examining the New York Historical Society copy, I noticed in the space next to May 20–21: "The Printer born the 30th, 1663." The position of the entry was evidently responsible for the mistake.

6. *An Address Delivered at the Celebration by the New York Historical Society, May 20, 1863, of the Two Hundredth Birth Day of Mr. William Bradford* (Albany, New York: J. Munsell, 1863).

7. Ibid., pp. 49ff.

8. *The Autobiography of Benjamin Franklin*, edited by Leonard W. Labaree et al. (New Haven: Yale University Press, 1964), p. 78.

9. Isaiah Thomas, *History of Printing in New York* (2 vols., 1810; reprint ed. in 1 vol., Barre, Massachusetts: Imprint Society, 1970), p. 461.

10. The correct date, 1691, is given by James Truslow Adams, *Provincial Society, 1690–1763* (New York: The Macmillan Company, 1927), p. 130.

11. *Daniel Leeds*, 1696 (October).

12. *Daniel Leeds*, 1712 (January).

13. Ibid., (February).

14. *Titan Leeds*, 1729 and after; *Felix Leeds*, 1730.

15. *Daniel Leeds*, 1706.

16. *Daniel Leeds*, 1706 (copy in John Carter Brown Library, Providence, Rhode Island).

17. *Daniel Leeds*, 1713.

18. *Daniel Leeds*, 1706 (preface).

19. *Daniel Leeds*, 1694.

20. *Daniel Leeds*, 1705.

21. *Daniel Leeds,* 1709.

22. *Titan Leeds,* 1722 (preface).

23. For the contents of a typical New York almanac in the decade before the Revolution, see Appendix B; also see the complete calendar verses in *Titan Leeds,* 1740, Chapter 8 above, pp. 100–102.

24. Cf *Titan Leeds,* 1714 (preface). But an entry on the August calendar in the almanac for 1715 states that he was born August 25, 1699.

25. *Titan Leeds,* 1715 (May).

26. *Titan Leeds,* 1714 (August).

27. The *Daniel Travis* almanacs, though without the Bradford imprint, have been ascribed to him. See Alexander J. Wall, *A List of New York Almanacs 1694–1850* (New York: The New York Public Library, 1921), p. 6.

28. William Harrison Bayles, *Old Taverns of New York* (New York: Frank Allaben Genealogical Company, 1915), pp. 49–52. Jacob Leisler, a German immigrant, was the leader of an anti-Catholic group in New York who failed in an attempt to seize the government of the province in 1689. After a trial for treason, he was hanged.

29. For example, *Titan Leeds,* 1731 and *Poor Richard,* 1734. Answers were sent in by many readers. In *Titan Leeds,* 1732, the names of winners included that of the Rev. James Wetmore of Trinity Church in New York and of Thomas Godfrey, Franklin's friend and the inventor of the mariner's quadrant.

30. In the preface to his almanac for 1762, Hutchins speaks of "my deceased master, Mr. Titan Leeds."

31. *Stearns Universal Kalendar* for 1784 mentions his recent death.

32. Preface to Gale's *New York Almanack* for 1747.

33. *Roger Sherman,* 1750.

34. *Roger More,* 1761 (preface).

35. *Hutchins,* 1762 (preface).

36. The imprint is torn off, but it was probably printed by Parker and Weyman, who printed the English *Thomas More* for that year. This unique copy is in the library of the New Jersey Historical Society in Newark.

37. The copy is in the library of the New York Historical Society. J. Parker and Co. printed it.

38. David McNeely Stauffer, *American Engravers upon Copper and Steel,* 2 vols. (New York: The Grolier Club, 1907), vol. 1, pp. 167–68.

39. Ibid., pp. 60–62.

40. Ibid., vol. 2, p. 80.

41. James Fowler, *On Mediaeval Representations of the Months and Seasons* (London, 1873), pp. 1ff.

42. In *Daniel Leeds,* 1713; *Titan Leeds,* 1714, 1720; *Thomas More,* 1765; and Gaine's *Universal Register,* 1782. One John Hyatt, a glass-founder, advertised in *Titan Leeds,* 1714 and 1720. The 1713 and 1720 advertisements were from Philadelphia, and the one in 1765 from New Jersey.

43. Thomas Wright, "History of Almanacs," *Macmillan's Magazine* 7 (1862–63), p. 183.

44. Advertised in *Daniel Leeds,* 1699 and 1700.

45. *The New-York Pocket Almanack,* 1763.

46. *Hutchins,* 1765

47. *The New-York Pocket Almanack,* 1766

48. Ibid.

49. Ibid.

50. *Hutchins,* 1765

51. *Daniel Leeds,* 1695.

52. *Titan Leeds,* 1731 and 1732.

53. *Titan Leeds,* 1718.

54. *New-York Pocket Almanack,* 1762 (New York Historical Society copy), November and December.

55. Ibid., 1776 (New York Historical Society copy), January.

56. Ibid., 1766 (New York Historical Society copy).

57. Ibid., 1775 (New York Historical Society copy).

Chapter Two

1. London, 1775, pp. 390–91.

2. Ibid., p. 419n.

3. *Roger More,* 1765.

4. Ibid., 1764.

5. *A Concise Account of North America* (London, 1765), p. 233.

6. Albert Keiser, *The Indian in American Literature* (New York: Oxford University Press, 1933), p. 26.

7. *Roger More,* 1769.

8. Ibid., 1770.

9. *Webster's Calendar,* 1793 (Albany, N.Y.).

10. Mary L. Booth, *History of the City of New York* (New York: W.R.C. Clarke & Co., 1859), p. 178.

11. Seymour Dunbar, *History of Travel in America* (1915; reprint ed., 4 vols., New York: Greenwood Press, 1968), vol. 1, p. 46.

12. See *The Journal of Madam Knight* (1704/1705) (reprint ed., Boston: D.R. Godine, 1972).

13. Dunbar, *Travel in America,* vol. 1, p. 222.

14. *New-York Pocket Almanack,* 1766.

15. Dunbar, *Travel in America,* vol. 1, pp. 182–84.

16. For example, *Roger More,* 1765.

17. *Hutchins,* 1757

18. *New-York Pocket Almanack,* 1774 and 1775.

19. Dunbar, *Travel in America,* vol. 1, p. 63.

Chapter Three

1. *Kalendarium Pennsilvaniense,* 1686.

2. *New-York Pocket Almanack,* 1779 and 1781.

3. Fred J. Perrine, "The Significance of the English and American Almanacs of the 17th and 18th Centuries" (Ph.D. diss., 2 vols., New York University, 1917), vol. 2, p. 151.

4. *Wing Improv'd,* 1764.

5. *Hutchins,* 1779.

6. Ibid.

7. Alice M. Earle, *Home Life in Colonial Days* (1898; reprint ed., New York: The Macmillan Company, 1899), p. 165.

8. *Thomas More,* 1761

9. *B. A. Philo-Astro,* 1723.

10. *Hutchins.* 1765.

11. *Roger More,* 1765.

12. *Hamilton's Itinerarium . . . 1744,* edited by Albert B. Hart (St. Louis, Missouri: W. K. Bixby, 1907), p. 179.

13. *Freeman,* 1771.

14. *Wing Reviv'd,* 1762.

15. *Daniel Leeds,* 1706.

16. *New-York Pocket Almanack,* 1757.

17. *The World Almanac . . . 1977* (New York, 1976), p. 955.

18. *New-York Pocket Almanack,* 1757; *Gaine's Universal Register,* 1775.

19. For example, *New-York Pocket Almanack,* 1764 and *Thomas More,* 1764.

20. Letter quoted by Esther Singleton, *Social New York under the Georges, 1714–1776* (1 vol., 1902; reprint ed., 2 vols., Port Washington, N. Y.: Ira J. Friedman, Inc., 1969), vol. 2, pp. 359–60.

21. Over the mantel-shelf of the taproom in an old tavern appeared this notice: "Gentlemen learning to spell are requested to use last week's news letter." Quoted by Alice M. Earle, *Stage-Coach and Tavern Days* (1900; reprint ed., New York: The Macmillan Company, 1930), p. 91.

22. In a Newport tavern. 1762, ibid., pp. 200ff.

23. Ibid., pp. 69–70.

24. *New-York Pocket Almanack,* 1766.

25. *Titan Leeds,* 1737.

26. *Gaine's Universal Register,* 1775.

27. The text followed is that of *The Papers of Benjamin Franklin,* edited by Leonard W. Labaree et al. (New Haven: Yale University Press, 1960), vol. 2, p. 226.

28. *Itinerarium . . . 1744,* p. 47.

29. *Daniel Leeds,* 1705.

30. *Hutchins,* 1790.

31. *Roger Sherman,* 1750.

32. *Hutchins,* 1762.

33. *Hutchins,* 1755 and 1760.

34. *Titan Leeds,* 1716.

35. Ibid., 1729.

36. *New-York Pocket Almanack,* 1766.

37. *Thomas More,* 1760.

Chapter Four

1. William Smith, *History of the Province of New York . . .* (London, 1757), p. 212.

2. Ibid.

3. Samuel Briggs, *. . . Nathaniel Ames, . . . 1726–1775* (Cleveland, Ohio: [Short & Forman], 1891), p. 361.

4. *Thomas More,* 1752.

5. Quoted by J. Thomas Scharf and Thompson Westcott, *History of Philadelphia,* 3 vols. (Philadelphia: L.H. Everts & Co., 1884), vol. 2, p. 1502.

6. *Hutchins,* 1784.

7. Ibid., 1765.

8. *Thomas More,* 1754.

9. *Titan Leeds,* 1715.

10. *Hutchins,* 1765.

11. *Roger More,* 1765.

12. Ibid., 1763

13. *Titan Leeds,* 1718 and 1734; *Frank Freeman,* 1772 (in prose).

14. *Father Hutchins,* 1790.

15. *Universal Kalendar,* 1784.

16. *Titan Leeds,* 1720.

17. *Father Hutchins Revived,* 1792

18. *Hutchins,* 1765.

19. *Titan Leeds,* 1733.

20. *Hutchins,* 1760.

21. *Thomas More,* 1760.

22. *Hutchins,* 1763.

23. *Thomas More,* 1760

24. *Roger More,* 1767

25. For example, the poem, "The Reformed Debauchee's Confession," in *Father Abraham*, 1759.

26. *Titan Leeds*, 1724.

27. *Hutchins*, 1757.

28. *Hutchins*, 1770

29. For example, *Frank Freman*, 1770.

30. *Hutchins*, 1770.

31. *Hutchins*, 1777.

32. Ibid.

33. For example, *Hutchins*, 1771; also in *Freebetter's* Connecticut Almanack, 1774 and *Poor Richard*, 1763.

34. *Hutchins*, 1775.

35. *Wing*, 1764.

36. For example, *Copernicus*, 1746; *Wing*, 1762; *Father Abraham*, 1759; *Hutchins*, 1766.

37. *Hutchins*, 1766.

38. *Titan Leeds*, 1719.

39. *Hutchins*, 1792.

Chapter Five

1. For example, Perrine, "English and American Almanacs," vol. 2, p. 78.

2. *Crackerbox Philosophers in American Humor and Satire* (New York: Columbia University Press, 1925), Introduction.

3. Cf. George Saintsbury, *The Peace of the Augustans* (London: G. Bell and Sons, Ltd., 1916), p. 377: "The Augustans were free-spoken, and to a certain extent also foul-spoken; but they were not, with the exception of Sterne, Williams, Stevenson, and one or two more, . . . dirty."

4. *Thomas More*, 1754.

5. Ibid., 1763

6. Facsimile by Frazier-Soye (Paris, 1925).

7. *Wing Reviv'd*, 1762.

8. *Hutchins*, 1761.

9. *Thomas More*, 1767.

10. *Loudon*, 1787.

11. Thelma L. Kellogg, "American Social Satire before 1800," 2 vols. (Ph.D. dissertation, Radcliffe, 1929), vol. 1, p. 175.

12. *Roger More*, 1764.

13. *Greenleaf*, 1792.

14. *Bickerstaff*, 1778

15. Singleton, *Social New York* (1969 reprint), vol. 2, p. 382.

16. *Roger More*, 1767.

17. *Freeman*, 1768.

18. *Hutchins*, 1769

Chapter Six

1. First suggested by John Gough, *History of the People called Quakers* (Dublin, 1790).

2. John W. Wallace, *Two Hundredth Birth Day of Mr. William Bradford* (Albany, N.Y., 1863), p. 54.

3. Ellis P. Oberholtzer, *Philadelphia: A History of the City and its People*, 4 vols. (Philadelphia: The S.J. Clarke Publishing Company, 1912), vol. 1, p. 58.

4. From a report to the Society, quoted in James Bowden, *History of the Society of Friends in America*, 2 vols. (London, 1850, 1854), vol. 2, p. 87.

5. Vernon L. Parrington, *Main Currents in American Thought*, 3 vols. in 1 (New York: Harcourt, Brace and Company, 1930), vol. 1, p. 21.

6. Quoted by Oberholtzer, *Philadelphia*, vol. 1, p. 58.

7. Wallace, *Mr. William Bradford*, p. 12.

8. W. Rogers, *Scourge for G. Whitehead*. Rogers was a Quaker of Bristol.

9. Quoted in *Collections of the Protestant Episcopal Historical Society for . . . 1851* (New York, 1851), p. 51.

10. *Titan Leeds*, 1727.

11. *Copernicus*, 1746.

12. *Nathaniel Ames*, 1752.

13. Perrine, "English and American Almanacs," vol. 2, p. 236.

14. *Roger More*, 1769.

15. *Hutchins*, 1775.

16. *Roger More*, 1762.

17. *Daniel Leeds*, 1699.

18. *Hutchins*, 1783

19. Austin B. Keep, *History of the New York Society Library* (New York: De Vinne Press, 1908), p. 54.

20. Fragment in the New York Historical Society.

21. *Roger More*, 1767.

22. Ibid., 1761.

23. Quoted by Paul Leicester Ford, ed., *The New England Primer* (New York: Dodd, Mead and Co., 1897), pp. 244, 246.

24. For example, *Hutchins*, 1773.

25. *Hutchins*, 1776.

26. A striking example is the contract signed by a teacher at Flatbush, Long Island, in 1682, in which he agreed not only to teach the children, but also to ring the church bell on Sundays, read the Bible at the service, lead in the singing, sometimes read the sermon, prepare the water for baptisms and the bread and wine for communion, sweep out the church, deliver funeral invitations, carry messages, dig graves occasionally, and visit and comfort the sick! From Alice M. Earle, *Child Life in Colonial Days* (1899; reprint, New York: The Macmillan Company 1929), p. 74.

27. Bayles, *Old Taverns of New York*, p. 173.

28. For example, *Hutchins*, 1775. Intemperance was a common subject of satire in newspapers and almanacs throughout the colonies. See Kellogg, "American Social Satire," vol. 2, pp. 452–62.

29. *Hutchins*, 1765

30. Kellogg, "American Social Satire," vol. 2, pp. 462–65.

Chapter Seven

1. Michael Kraus, *Intercolonial Aspects of American Culture* (1928; reprint, New York: Octagon Books, 1964), pp. 170–71.

2. *Roger More*, 1764; *Thomas More*, 1760, 1766; *Hutchins*, 1772, 1776.

3. *Thomas More*, 1767, 1768; *Rivington*, 1774; *Hutchins*, 1776.

4. *Freeman*, 1768; *Hutchins*, 1774 (2nd ed.).

5. *Hutchins*, 1763, 1772; *Roger More*, 1764; *Freeman*, 1769, 1771.

6. *Hutchins*, 1760, 1767; *Freeman*, 1770.

7. *Daniel Leeds*, 1709; *Hutchins*, 1762, 1767, 1773.

8. *Thomas More*, 1767; *Hutchins*, 1773, 1774 (2nd ed.), 1775.

9. *Hutchins*, 1760.

10. *Hutchins*, 1765; *Freeman* 1769; *Roger More*, 1770.

11. *Hutchins*, 1774 (2nd ed.).

12. *Titan Leeds*, 1742; *Roger More*, 1770.

13. *Thomas More*, 1767.

14. *Father Hutchins Revived,* 1790.
15. *Hutchins,* 1773, 1775.
16. *Hutchins,* 1773, 1775; *Rivington,* 1775.
17. *Hutchins,* 1788.
18. *Thomas More,* 1762, 1765; *Hutchins,* 1765.
19. *Hutchins,* 1773.
20. *Thomas More,* 1750, 1752, 1764; *Freeman,* 1770.
21. *Hutchins,* 1769, 1774 (2nd ed.).
22. *Freeman,* 1770.
23. *Thomas More,* 1755.
24. Ibid., 1763.
25. *Thomas More,* 1767; *Hutchins,* 1769, 1772.
26. Hutchins, 1769.
27. *Poor Will,* 1786.
28. *Hutchins,* 1763, 1775.
29. *Titan Leeds,* 1742; Roger More, 1771.
30. *Roger More,* 1763.
31. *Thomas More,* 1764.
32. *Roger More,* 1764; *Thomas More,* 1768; *Hutchins,* 1769, 1772, 1773, 1774 (2nd ed.).
33. *Hutchins,* 1775.
34. "Diary of Samuel Sewall," *Massachusetts Historical Society Collections,* 5th ser. 7 (1881): 31.
35. *Thomas More,* 1749.
36. *Jesse Parsons,* 1757.
37. *Titan Leeds,* 1726, 1734; *Roger Sherman,* 1753.
38. *Jesse Parsons,* 1757; *Roger More,* 1758.
39. *Freeman,* 1767.
40. *Roger More,* 1771
41. *B. A. Philo-Astro,* 1723.
42. *Hutchins,* 1774 (2nd ed.). 1775, 1776.
43. Francis R. Packard, *History of Medicine in the United States* (1931; reprint, 2 vols., New York: Hafner Publishing Company, 1963), vol. 1, pp. 276–77.
44. Ibid., p. 273.
45. Fielding H. Garrison, *Introduction to the History of Medicine,* 3rd ed. (Philadelphia: W.B. Saunders Company, 1922), p. 423.
46. *Thomas More,* 1760; *Hutchins,* 1762, 1769, 1772, 1773; *Freeman,* 1768, 1770; *New-York and Country,* 1776.
47. *Roger More,* 1756, 1771; *Thomas More,* 1760, 1764, 1768; *Hutchins,* 1762, 1772; *Freeman,* 1768; *New-York and Country,* 1776.
48. *Thomas More,* 1761; *Hutchins,* 1762, 1763, 1770; *Roger More,* 1770.
49. *Freeman,* 1768; *Thomas More,* 1768; *Hutchins,* 1769, 1773, 1775; *Roger More,* 1769; *Rivington,* 1775.
50. *Thomas More,* 1761, 1768; *Freeman,* 1768; *Hutchins,* 1771, 1774 (2nd ed.); *Roger More,* 1771; *Rivington,* 1775.
51. *Thomas More,* 1755; *Freeman,* 1768, 1770; *Hutchins,* 1769; *Roger More,* 1769, 1771; *Meanwell,* 1774.
52. *Freeman,* 1768, 1770; *Hutchins,* 1769; *Roger More,* 1769, 1771; *Meanwell,* 1774.
53. *Hutchins,* 1760, 1773; *Freeman,* 1768, 1770; *Thomas More,* 1768.
54. *Hutchins,* 1765, 1767, 1768; *Roger More,* 1771.
55. *Thomas More,* 1750; *Hutchins,* 1769, 1773; *Meanwell,* 1774; *New-York and Country,* 1776.
56. *Thomas More,* 1750, 1768.
57. *Freeman,* 1768; *Hutchins,* 1770; *Meanwell,* 1774; *New-York and Country,* 1776.
58. *Hutchins,* 1774 (2nd ed.), 1775, 1776; *Rivington,* 1774.
59. *Thomas More,* 1760, 1764, 1766; *Freeman,* 1768.
60. *Hutchins,* 1764; *Thomas More,* 1766; *Freeman,* 1768.

61. *Thomas More*, 1764, 1767; *Hutchins*, 1769; *New-York and Country*, 1776.

62. For example, *Roger More*, 1756, draws on the fifth volume of *Edinburgh Medical Essays* for a receipt for dysentery.

63. *Thomas More*, 1750

64. Ibid., 1758.

65. Ibid., 1760.

66. *Pennsylvania Magazine of History and Biography* 40 (1916): 475ff.

67. *Hutchins*, 1769, 1772.

68. *New-York Pocket Almanack*, 1763

69. Ibid., 1766.

70. *Hutchins*, 1768.

71. *Daniel Leeds*, 1694.

72. Ibid., 1708, 1709, 1713.

73. *The Dead Man's Almanack*, 1744.

74. *William Birkett*, 1738.

75. Edward J. Young, "Subjects for Master's Degree in Harvard College from 1655 to 1791," *Proceedings of the Massachusetts Historical Society* 18 (1880–81): 132.

76. *Ames*, 1747, in Briggs, *Nathaniel Ames*, pp. 198–99.

77. *Copernicus*, 1746, 1747.

78. *Thomas More*, 1748.

79. *W. Jones*, 1750.

80. Ibid.

81. *Hutchins*, 1753

Chapter Eight

1. *Daniel Leeds*, 1708 (May–August).

2. *Titan Leeds*, 1719.

3. Ibid., 1724. This date would indicate that Titan Leeds, rather than Nathaniel Ames, as is commonly held, should be credited with having introduced Dryden to the colonies.

4. *B. A. Philo-Astro*, 1723.

5. *Daniel Leeds*, 1710; *B. A. Philo-Astro*, 1723.

6. *Felix Leeds*, 1727; *Titan Leeds*, 1733.

7. *Roger Sherman*, 1753; *Hutchins*, 1755, 1758; *Jesse Parsons*, 1757; *Mark Time*, 1774.

8. *Hutchins*, 1769 (modernized).

9. *Freeman*, 1768.

10. *Roger Sherman*, 1753; *Thomas More*, 1760.

11. *Roger Sherman*, 1754; *Thomas More*, 1768; *Hutchins*, 1760; *Freeman*, 1770.

12. *Roger More*, 1762; *Hutchins*, 1763.

13. *Roger More*, 1765.

14. *Freeman*, 1767.

15. *Roger More*, 1758, 1770.

16. *Freeman*, 1771.

17. *Father Hutchins*, 1776.

18. Paul L. Ford (*Poor Richard*), Samuel Briggs (*Nathaniel Ames*), and Caroline G. Hogue ("Early American Almanac"). See Bibliography.

19. *Poor Robin*, 1741.

20. George L. Kittredge, *Old Farmer and His Almanack* (Cambridge: Harvard University Press, 1904), p. 32.

21. For example, *Hutchins*, 1756.

22. *Daniel Leeds*, 1699; *Titan Leeds*, 1716; *Poor Richard*, 1744; *Hutchins*, 1777.

23. Perrine, "English and American Almanac," (2 vols.) vol. 1, p. 274.

24. *Hutchins*, 1766.

25. *Bickerstaff*, 1779.

26. *Hutchins*, 1758. Cf. Hadrian's famous lyric, "Animula."

27. *Daniel Leeds*, 1697.

28. *Titan Leeds*, 1731.

29. *Freeman*, 1769.

30. For example, *Freeman*, 1771: "Edwin and Emma."

31. *Titan Leeds*, 1719.

32. *Kalendar* for 1508, in Perrine, "English and American Almanac," (2 vols.) vol. 2, pp. 39–48.

33. *Daniel Leeds*, 1711; *Roger Sherman*, 1753; *Wing Reviv'd*, 1762; *Roger More*, 1763; *Improv'd Wing*, 1764; *Thomas More*, 1768; *Hutchins*, 1775.

34. *Roger More*, 1756; *Father Abraham*, 1759.

35. *Thomas More*, 1748.

36. For example, *Thomas More*, 1753; *Hutchins*, 1770, 1772, 1774.

37. Anecdote of Leonidas, *Father Hutchins*, 1776; of King Poltis, *Hutchins*, 1769; of Vespasian and the Senator, *Hutchins*, 1776; of Pericles and the Philosopher, *Hutchins*, 1769.

38. *Hutchins*, 1776.

39. Frank Luther Mott, *History of American Magazines*, 5 vols. (Cambridge: Harvard University Press, 1957, 1966–1968), vol. 1, pp. 42–43.

40. *Freeman*, 1770.

41. *Hutchins*, 1760, 1765, 1767, 1770, 1775; *Freeman*, 1769; *Meanwell*, 1774.

42. *Daniel Leeds*, 1705.

43. *Thomas More*, 1763.

44. The reader will find a great many of the sources listed in George L. Apperson, *English Proverbs and Proverbial Phrases* (London: J.M. Dent & Sons, 1929).

45. *Titan Leeds*, 1742: *Experientia docet* (Experience teaches.). B. A. *Philo-Astro*, 1723: *Non vivas ut edas, sed edas ut vivere possis* (Do not live to eat, but eat to live.).

46. *Daniel Leeds*, 1694.

47. *Roger More*, 1764.

48. Ibid., 1756.

49. *Daniel Leeds*, 1709.

50. *Titan Leeds*, 1734; *Poor Richard*, 1733.

51. *Daniel Leeds*, 1709.

52. Ibid., 1710

53. Ibid.

54. *Thomas More*, 1753.

55. *Copernicus*, 1745; *Whittemore*, 1719 (Boston).

56. *Daniel Leeds*, 1695.

57. *Titan Leeds*, 1716.

58. Ibid., 1724.

59. *Roger More*, 1764.

60. *Daniel Leeds*, 1694. Cf. "Whip Heretics, and eat their orthodox Cattel," in James Franklin's *Rhode Island Almanack*, 1728.

61. *Daniel Leeds*, 1704.

62. *Hutchins*, 1763.

63. *Roger More*, 1765.

64. *New-York and Country*, 1776

65. *Hutchins*, 1755.

66. *Daniel Leeds*, 1708.

67. *Titan Leeds*, 1715.

68. *Daniel Leeds*, 1710.

69. *Titan Leeds*, 1734.

70. *Hutchins*, 1763

71. Ibid., 1783

72. Ibid.

73. *Daniel Leeds*, 1709.

74. *Hutchins,* 1766; *Poor Richard Improved,* 1753.
75. *Daniel Leeds,* 1700.
76. *Titan Leeds,* 1739.
77. *Felix Leeds,* 1727.
78. *Daniel Leeds,* 1707.
79. Ibid., 1709. Cf. "Fine linnen, girls and gold so bright Chuse not to take by candle light," *Poor Richard,* 1737.
80. *Daniel Leeds,* 1710.
81. *Titan Leeds,* 1730.
82. Ibid., 1740.
83. *Copernicus,* 1745.
84. *Hutchins,* 1765.
85. *Hutchins,* 1765; *Freeman,* 1771.
86. *Daniel Leeds,* 1712.
87. *B. A. Philo-Astro,* 1723.
88. *Titan Leeds,* 1734.
89. *Daniel Leeds,* 1704.
90. *Titan Leeds,* 1718.
91. *Daniel Leeds,* 1706.
92. *Titan Leeds,* 1724.
93. *Daniel Leeds,* 1707.
94. Ibid.
95. Ibid., 1709.
96. Ibid., 1712.
97. Ibid., 1713.
98. *Titan Leeds,* 1717.
99. Ibid., 1719.
100. Ibid., 1724.
101. Ibid., 1733.
102. *Hutchins,* 1762.
103. Ibid., 1766.
104. Ibid., 1771.
105. *Roger More,* 1762.
106. *Freeman,* 1770.
107. *Daniel Leeds,* 1700.
108. Ibid., 1705.
109. Ibid., 1710.
110. *Titan Leeds,* 1726; *Copernicus,* 1745.
111. *Titan Leeds,* 1734.
112. *Copernicus,* 1745.
113. *Thomas More,* 1750; *Hutchins,* 1765.
114. *Thomas More,* 1763.
115. *Hutchins,* 1766.
116. Ibid.
117. Ibid.
118. *Freeman,* 1769.
119. *Hutchins,* 1770.
120. Ibid., 1764.
121. *B. A. Philp-Astro,* 1723.

Chapter Nine

1. Letter to H. Niles, February 13, 1818, in *Works of John Adams,* edited by Charles Francis Adams, 10 vols. (Boston: Little, Brown and Company, 1850–1856), vol. 10, pp.

282ff. [Reprint, Freeport, N.Y.: Books for Libraries Press, 1969].

2. Its first line: "Awake yee westerne Nymphs, arise and sing."

3. *Roger More,* 1764; *Hutchins,* 1772, 1774 (2nd ed.).

4. *Social New York,* 2 vols. (New York, 1969), vol. 2, p. 375.

5. Robert Rogers, *Account of North America,* p. 71.

6. *Thomas More,* 1768 (preface).

7. The text is that in *The Papers of Benjamin Franklin,* edited by Leonard W. Labaree et al. (New Haven: Yale University Press, 1963), vol. 7, pp. 84–85.

8. *Freeman,* 1768.

9. Reprinted in *Mark Time,* 1774.

10. *Daniel Leeds,* 1709.

11. *Roger More,* 1757. Similar criticisms appeared in his almanac for 1758 and in *Hutchins,* 1758.

12. In a list of privateers from New York, printed in *Roger More,* 1758.

13. *Roger More,* 1757.

14. James T. Adams, *Provincial Society* (New York, 1927), p. 317.

15. See Chapter 6 above, pp. 80–81.

16. Quoted by Matthew A. Stickney, "Almanacs and Their Authors," *Historical Collections of the Essex Institute* 8 (1868): 161.

17. Peter Kalm, *Travels into North America,* translated by John R. Forster (1770; reprint ed., 1 vol., Barre, Massachusetts: Imprint Society, 1972), p. 138.

18. For example, *Daniel Leeds,* 1706; *Thomas More,* 1753; *Poor Tom,* 1757 (pocket almanac); *Gaine's Universal Register,* 1775.

19. *Poor Tom,* 1757.

20. The actual number was fewer than 13 million.

21. Samuel Briggs, *Nathaniel Ames,* p. 286.

22. Ibid., p. 372.

23. *Thomas More,* 1766 (preface)

24. *Hutchins,* 1766.

25. *Freeman,* 1769; *Roger More,* 1769.

26. *Roger More,* 1771.

27. Ibid., 1770.

28. *Nathaniel Ames,* 1766.

29. *Freeman,* 1770.

30. *Hutchins,* 1772.

31. New York Historical Society copy.

32. New York Historical Society copy.

Selected Bibliography

Primary Sources

Bates, Albert Carlos. "Checklist of Connecticut Almanacs, 1709–1850." *American Antiquarian Society Proceedings*, n. s. 24 (1914), 93–215.

Chapin, Howard Millar. "Checklist of Rhode Island Almanacs, 1643–1850." *American Antiquarian Society Proceedings*, n. s. 25 (1915), 19–54.

Drake, Milton, compiler. *Almanacs of the United States*. 2 vols. New York: The Scarecrow Press, Inc., 1962.

Evans, Charles and Shipton, Clifford K., editors. *American Bibliography 1639–1820*. 13 vols. New York: Peter Smith, 1941–62. Index, vol. 14, by R. P. Bristol. Gloucester, Massachusetts: Peter Smith, 1967.

Heartman, Charles Frederick. *Preliminary Checklist of Almanacs Printed in New Jersey Prior to 1850*. Metuchen, N.J., 1929.

Morrison, Hugh Alexander. *Checklist of American Almanacs 1639–1800*. Washington, D.C.: Government Printing Office, 1907.

Nichols, Charles Lemuel. "Checklist of Maine, New Hampshire and Vermont Almanacs." *American Antiquarian Society Proceedings*, n. s. 38 (1928), 63–163.

Nichols, Charles Lemuel. "Notes on the Almanacs of Massachusetts." *American Antiquarian Society Proceedings*, n. s. 22 (1912), 15–134.

Wall, Alexander J. *A List of New York Alamancs 1694–1850*. New York: The New York Public Library, 1921.

Webber, Mabel L. "South Carolina Almanacs." *South Carolina Historical and Genealogical Magazine*, 15 (1914), 73–81.

Secondary Sources

1. Background

Adams, James Truslow. *Provincial Society, 1690–1763*. New York: The Macmillan Company, 1927.

Andrews, Charles M. *Colonial Folkways; A Chronicle of American Life in the Reign of the Georges*. New Haven: Yale University Press, 1919.

Apperson, G. L. *English Proverbs and Proverbial Phrases*. London: J. M. Dent & Sons, 1929.

Bayles, William Harrison. *Old Taverns of New York*. New York: Frank Allaben Genealogical Company, 1915.

Boorstin, Daniel J. *The Americans; The Colonial Experience*. New York: Random House, 1958.

Booth, Mary L. *History of the City of New York*. New York: W.R.C. Clarke & Co., 1859.

Bosworth, F. H. "The Doctor in Old New York." *Historic New York*, Second Series, 1897. Edited by Maud W. Goodwin et al. Reprint, 2 vols. in 4. Port Washington,

N.Y.: Ira J. Friedman, Inc., 1969. Vol. 4, pp. 279–317.

"The Bradford Bi-Centenary." *The Critic* (New York), 22 (1893), 236f.

Brown, Henry Collins. *The Story of Old New York.* New York: E. P. Dutton & Co., 1934.

Chitwood, Oliver P. *A History of Colonial America.* Third Edition. New York: Harper & Brothers, 1961.

Colden, Cadwallader. *The History of the Five Indian Nations . . . of New York in America.* 1727. Reprint, Ithaca, N. Y.: Cornell University Press (Great Seal Books), 1958.

Dexter, F. B. "Estimates of Population in the American Colonies." *American Antiquarian Society Proceedings,* n. s. 5 (1887–88), 22–50.

Dumond, Dwight L. *Anti-Slavery; The Crusade for Freedom in America.* Ann Arbor: University of Michigan Press, 1961.

Dunbar, Seymour. *A History of Travel in America.* 1915. Reprint, 4 vols. New York: Greenwood Press, 1968.

Eames, Wilberforce. "The First Year of Printing in New York, May, 1693–April, 1694." *Bulletin of the New York Public Library,* 32 (1928), 3–24.

Earle, Alice Morse. *Child Life in Colonial Days.* 1899. Reprint, New York: The Macmillan Company, 1929.

Earle, Alice Morse. *Colonial Dames and Good Wives.* Boston: Houghton, Mifflin & Company, 1895. [Reprint, New York: Ungar, 1962].

Earle, Alice Morse. *Colonial Days in Old New York.* 1896. Reprint, Port Washington, N.Y.: Ira J. Friedman, Inc., 1965.

Earle, Alice Morse. *Home Life in Colonial Days.* 1898. Reprint, New York: The Macmillan Company, 1899.

Earle, Alice Morse. *Stage-Coach and Tavern Days.* 1900. Reprint, New York: The Macmillan Company, 1930.

Flick, Alexander C., ed. *History of the State of New York.* 10 vols. New York: Columbia University Press, 1933–37. (Vols. 1–3).

Ford, Paul Leicester, ed. *The Journals Of Hugh Gaine Printer.* 2 vols. New York: Dodd, Mead & Company, 1902.

Franklin, John H. *From Slavery to Freedom; A History of Negro Americans.* 3rd ed. rev. and enl. New York: Alfred A. Knopf, 1967.

Garland, Hamlin. *A Son of the Middle Border.* 1917. Edited by Henry M. Christman. New York: The Macmillan Company, 1962. (Chapter 12).

Handlin, Oscar. *The Uprooted.* 2d ed. enl. Boston: Little, Brown, 1973.

Heimert, Alan. *Religion and the American Mind; From the Great Awakening to the Revolution.* Cambridge: Harvard University Press, 1966.

Hildeburn, Charles S. R. *Sketches of Printers and Printing in Colonial New York.* New York: Dodd, Mead & Company, 1895.

Hofstadter, Richard. *America at 1750; A Social Portrait.* New York: Alfred A. Knopf, 1971.

Holliday, Carl. *The Wit and Humor of Colonial Days (1607–1800).* Philadelphia: J.B. Lippincott Company, 1912.

Holliday, Carl. *Woman's Life in Colonial Days.* Boston: Cornhill Publishing Co., 1922.

The Journal of Madam Knight. (Sarah Kemble Knight). 1704/05. Reprint. Introd. by Malcolm Freiberg. Boston: D. R. Godine, 1972.

Kalm, Peter. *Travels into North America.* Tr. by J. R. Forster. 2 vols. 1770. Reprint, 1 vol. Barre, Massachusetts: Imprint Society, 1972.

Keiser, Albert. *The Indian in American Literature.* New York: Oxford University Press, 1933.

Kellogg, Thelma L. "American Social Satire before 1800." 2 vols. Ph.D. diss. Radcliffe, 1929.

Kraus, Michael. *Intercolonial Aspects of American Culture on the Eve of the Revolution. . . .* 1928. Reprint, New York: Octagon Books, 1964.

Lyndoe, Edward. *Astrology for Everyone.* New rev. ed. New York: Dutton, 1970.

Major, Ralph Herman. *A History of Medicine.* 2 vols. Springfield, Illinois: Charles C. Thomas, [1954].

Morison, Samuel Eliot. "Squire Ames and Doctor Ames." *The New England Quarterly*, 1 (1928), 5–31.
Osgood, Herbert L. *The American Colonies in the Eighteenth Century.* 4 vols. 1924. Reprint, Gloucester, Massachusetts: Peter Smith, 1958.
Parrington, Vernon Louis. *Main Currents in American Thought . . . from the Beginnings to 1920.* 3 vols. in 1. New York: Harcourt, Brace and Company, 1930. (Vol. 1, pp. 131–78).
Pearce, Alfred J. *The Text-Book of Astrology.* London: Cousins and Co., 1889. 2nd ed., 1911.
Rogers, Robert. *A Concise Account of North America.* London, 1765.
Rossiter, Clinton L. *Seedtime of the Republic.* New York: Harcourt, Brace, 1953.
Savelle, Max. *The Colonial Origins of American Thought.* Princeton, N. J.: D. Van Nostrand Company, Inc., 1964.
Schlesinger, Arthur Meier, Sr. *New Viewpoints in American History.* New York: The Macmillan Company, 1922.
Singleton, Esther. *Social New York under the Georges, 1714–1776.* 1902. Reprint, 2 vols. Port Washington, N. Y.: Ira J. Friedman, Inc., 1969.
Tandy, Jennette. *Crackerbox Philosophers in American Humor and Satire.* New York: Columbia University Press, 1925.
Thomas, Isaiah. *The History of Printing in America.* 2 vols. 1810. Edited by Marcus A. McCorison from the 2d ed. vol. Barre, Massachusetts: Imprint Society, 1970.
Tyler, Moses Coit. *A History of American Literature, 1607–1765.* 1878, rev. 1897. With a new foreword by Perry Miller. New York: Collier Books, 1962.
Ver Steeg, Clarence L. *The Formative Years 1607–1763.* New York: Hill and Wang, 1964.
Wechsler, Louis K. *Benjamin Franklin: American and World Educator.* Boston: Twayne Publishers, 1976. (Pages 61–67, 105–106).
Wright, Louis B. *The Cultural Life of the American Colonies 1607–1763.* New York: Harper Brothers, 1957.
Wyllie, Irvin G. *The Self-Made Man in America.* New Brunswick, New Jersey: Rutgers University Press, 1954.

2. Writings on Almanacs
Albee, John. "Dudley Leavitt's New Hampshire Almanac." *The New England Magazine*, n. s. 17 (1898), 545–55.
Bates, Albert Carlos. "Connecticut Almanacs of the Last Century." *The Connecticut Quarterly*, 4 (1898), 408–16.
Bosanquet, Eustace F. "English Seventeenth-Century Almanacks." *The Library*, 4th series 10 (1930), 361–97.
Briggs, Samuel. *The Essays, Humor, and Poems of Nathaniel Ames, Father and Son . . . 1726–1775.* Cleveland, Ohio: [Short & Forman], 1891.
Briggs, Samuel. *The Origin and Development of the Almanac.* Cleveland, Ohio: Leader Printing Company, 1887. (Western Reserve Historical Society Tract No. 69).
Brigham, Clarence S. *An Account of American Almanacs and Their Value for Historical Study.* Worcester, Massachusetts: American Antiquarian Society, 1925.
Einfrank, Aaron. "The Lure of Old Almanacs." *Hobbies*, 63 (June 1952), 130–31.
Ford, Paul Leicester, ed. *The Prefaces, Proverbs, and Poems of Benjamin Franklin. (Poor Richard, 1733–1758).* New York: [G. P. Putnam's Sons], 1890.
Greenough, Chester Noyes. "New England Almanacs, 1766–1775, and the American Revolution." *American Antiquarian Society Proceedings*, 45 (1935), 288–316.
Hogue, Caroline G. "The Early American Almanac as a Literary Vehicle." Master of arts thesis. George Washington University, 1930.
"Items from an Interleaved Copy of Ames's Almanac for 1746, Belonging to Rev. John Cushing." *The New England Historical and Genealogical Register*, 19 (1865), 237–41.
Jerabek, Esther. "Almanacs as Historical Sources." *Minnesota History*, 15 (1934), 444–49.

Kittredge, George Lyman. *The Old Farmer and His Almanack*. Cambridge: Harvard University Press, 1904.

Littlefield, George E. "Notes on the Calendar and the Almanac." *American Antiquarian Society Proceedings*, n. s. 24 (1914), 11–64.

"The Neglect of the Almanac." *Scribner's Magazine*, 67 (1920), 120–21.

Nichols, Charles Lemuel. "Notes on the Almanacs of Massachusetts." *American Antiquarian Society Proceedings*, n. s. 22 (1912), 15–134

"Notes from the Rev. Samuel Cooper's Interleaved Almanacs of 1764 and 1769." Edited by Frederick Tuckerman. *The New England Historical and Genealogical Register*, 55 (1901), 145–49.

Page, Alfred B. "John Tulley's Almanacks, 1687–1702." *Colonial Society of Massachusetts Publications*, 13 (1910), 207–23.

Paltsits, Victor Hugo. "The Almanacs of Roger Sherman." *American Antiquarian Society Proceedings*, n. s. 18 (1907), pp. 217ff.

The Papers of Benjamin Franklin. Edited by Leonard W. Laboree and Whitfield J. Bell, Jr. New Haven: Yale University Press, 1959–. Vol. 1, pp. 280–318. (*Poor Richard*, 1733).

Perrine, Fred J. "The Significance of the English and American Almanac of the 17th and 18th Centuries." 2 vols. Doctoral dissertation. New York University, 1917.

Robbins, L. H. "Counselor and Friend." *New York Times Magazine* (March 9, 1947), 18.

Robinson, Henry Morton. "The Almanac." *The Bookman*, 75 (1932), 218–24.

Rosenbach, A. S. W. "Old Almanacs and Prognostications." *Saturday Evening Post*, 207 (June 8, 1935), 10–11, 90–95.

Sagendorph, Robb. *America and her Almanacs: Wit, Wisdom & Weather 1639–1970*. Dublin, New Hampshire: Yankee, Inc. and Boston: Little, Brown, 1970.

Stickney, Matthew A. "Almanacs and Their Authors." *Essex Institute Historical Collections*. Vol 8 (1868) and vol. 14 (1878).

The Writings of Benjamin Franklin. Edited by Albert Henry Smyth. 10 vols. New York: The Macmillan Company, 1905. Vols. 1–3. (*Poor Richard* almanacs)

Index